Kay Warrington grew up in Swansea and, after living in west Wales and mid-W[cut] *now lives in Ystalyfera, in the Swansea valley. She taught Science and Biology for nearly 20 years, was ordained deacon in 1995 and worked with her husband Gwyn as an NSM curate for six years prior to his death, early in 2005. She has been Diocesan Children's Officer for Swansea and Brecon for nine years and also Provincial Children and Families Officer since 2000.*

Important information

Photocopying permission

The right to photocopy material in *Play and Pray through Lent* is granted for the pages that contain the photocopying clause: 'Reproduced with permission from *Play and Pray through Lent* published by BRF 2005 (ISBN 1 84101 392 7)', so long as reproduction is for use in a teaching situation by the original purchaser. The right to photocopy material is not granted for anyone other than the original purchaser without written permission from BRF.

The Copyright Licensing Agency (CLA)

If you are resident in the UK and you have a photocopying licence with the Copyright Licensing Agency (CLA), please check the terms of your licence. If your photocopying request falls within the terms of your licence, you may proceed without seeking further permission. If your request exceeds the terms of your CLA licence, please contact the CLA directly with your request. Copyright Licensing Agency, 90 Tottenham Court Rd, London W1T 4LP. Tel 020 7631 5555; fax 020 7631 5500; email cla@cla.co.uk; web www.cla.co.uk. The CLA will provide photocopying authorization and royalty fee information on behalf of BRF.

BRF is a Registered Charity (No. 233280)

Text copyright © Kay Warrington 2005
Illustrations copyright © Lorna Kent 2005
The author asserts the moral right
to be identified as the author of this work

Published by
The Bible Reading Fellowship
First Floor, Elsfield Hall
15–17 Elsfield Way, Oxford OX2 8FG
Website: www.brf.org.uk

ISBN 1 84101 392 7
First published 2005
10 9 8 7 6 5 4 3 2 1 0
All rights reserved

Acknowledgments
All scripture quotations are taken from the Contemporary English
Version of the Bible published by HarperCollins Publishers, copyright
© 1991, 1992, 1995 American Bible Society.

A catalogue record for this book is available from the British Library

Printed in Singapore by Craft Print International Ltd

PLAY and PRAY through Lent

A Family resource:
Stories and activities to use with children at home

Edited by Kay Warrington

*This book is dedicated to Gwyn,
who lived through this project with me*

Acknowledgments

Contributors to this book include past and present members of the Church in Wales Children's Committee.

Lynn Chambers
Susan Collingbourne
John Davis
Leslie Francis
Dennis Richards
Marion Richards
Tegid Roberts
Ann Smitham
Kay Warrington
Nia Catrin Williams

Comments from field test

All the material in this book has been field tested prior to publication. For your interest and encouragement, here are some of the comments that were subsequently fed back to the editor.

'The material certainly helped children to think throughout Lent and to make more sense of it all.' *(St Bride's, Major-Llandaff)*

'My four- and six-year-olds got a lot out of it. It filled the ten-minute slot before bedtime really well—a good focus rather than just reading a Bible story.' *(St Andrew's, Clevelys, Blackburn)*

'We used the project in a midweek 30-minute lunchtime session at our local primary school. We adapted it to use all of the week's activities and talking points in one session. We had 20 to 30 children at most sessions—aged between 4 and 7. The children liked the visual display and listened well.' *(Rhossili, Swansea and Brecon)*

'My children enjoyed the activities and were very proud of the story cloth, which was laid out throughout the course and after Easter at home. It reinforced what was learnt in school and Sunday school.' *(Family from Christ Church School, Swansea and Brecon)*

'We used the material as a Lent project in Sunday school and it proved to be a good focus for the children aged 3 to 13 years.' *(Llanfrechfa, Monmouth)*

'We used the material in school with a Year 1/2 class of 30 children, none of whom go to church. Children really enjoyed the project and there were encouraging comments from the parents. The children empathized with the characters, bringing lots of expression and language into their response. A wonderful experience for both the children and myself.' *(St Paul's, Nelson, Blackburn)*

Contents

Foreword 8
Introduction 9

Year A

Week One: Jesus in the desert (Matthew 4:10) 10
Week Two: Jesus talks about eternal life (John 3:16) 12
Week Three: Jesus talks about living water (John 4:14) 14
Week Four: Jesus shows the power of God (John 9:3) 16
Week Five: Jesus brings new life from death (John 11:25) 18
Week Six: Jesus shares the last supper with his friends (Matthew 26:26) 20
Holy Week and Easter Day: Jesus is alive (Matthew 28:10) 22

Year B

Week One: Jesus in the desert (Mark 1:12–13) 24
Week Two: Jesus invites people to follow him (Mark 8:34) 26
Week Three: Jesus clears the temple (John 2:16) 28
Week Four: Jesus, the way to life (John 3:15) 30
Week Five: Jesus talks about his death (John 12:32) 32
Week Six: Jesus rides into Jerusalem (Mark 11:9) 34
Holy Week and Easter Day: Jesus is alive (Mark 16:6) 36

Year C

Week One: Jesus in the desert (Luke 4:1–2a) 38
Week Two: Jesus is warned about his death (Luke 13:31) 40
Week Three: Jesus gives us a second chance (Luke 13:9) 42
Week Four: Jesus talks about love and forgiveness (Luke 15:32) 44
Week Five: Jesus talks about his death (John 12:7) 46
Week Six: Jesus dies on the cross (Luke 23:46) 48
Holy Week and Easter Day: Jesus is alive (John 20:18) 50

Songs for the week

Year A 54
Year B 61
Year C 68

Templates

Year A 76
Year B 85
Year C 90

Foreword

Those of us who work with children and young people in parishes struggle at times with issues of difficult themes, subjects and messages, as well as the appropriateness of methods and words and how to make our Christian teaching meaningful and engaging. There are also questions about creating effective links between the church and the home, aiming to encourage continuity in teaching and learning, and creating opportunities to enhance and affirm this continuity among all ages together.

In *Play and Pray through Lent*, Kay Warrington provides a comprehensive yet simple guide to this penitential season in the Church's year. The creative programme links to the Revised Common Lectionary Gospel readings for each Sunday in Lent, covering the three-year cycle. Through each week, the children, with their families or group leaders, are encouraged to focus on the teaching for the week, engage with the activities and be guided in preparation for worship each Sunday. The natural links that bring the teaching and worship together help to create and encourage positive, meaningful responses and engagement. The exciting ideas for use of the increasingly popular *Godly Play*, the positive encouragement to create a 'special' or 'sacred' space, and the expectation of extending the teaching integrally with the Sunday worship, bring freshness and attract interest in making use of this new resource.

Parishes and individuals in Blackburn Diocese felt privileged to be invited to take part in piloting this material. They enthused about the children's active involvement in the learning programme, and also their willingness to develop it within the wider sphere of worship together in bigger groups, be they church congregations or community gatherings. The challenge to readers now is to make active use of this book with children and young people in appropriate groups, develop the ideas and be open to learning and sharing together. The guaranteed results will include more positive teaching and learning, with the children's ideas centred in a wider experience of listening and learning together, and a better understanding of the significance of worshipping together. I hope you will enjoy responding to the challenge.

Mary A.R. Binks
Children's Work Adviser, Blackburn Diocese 1991–2005

Introduction

Play and Pray through Lent links the world of the child with the great Lenten themes of the Church. This innovative programme, based on the Revised Common Lectionary, suggests ways in which children can engage with the story at home, by exploring themes from the Gospels and preparing for the Sunday worship of their local church.

The material is based on the methodology of *Godly Play*, using story cloths and simple visuals to tell the story. *Godly Play* is a teaching method developed by Jerome Berryman in the United States. Play is nature's way of extending a child's horizons and understanding of life. *Godly Play* draws on this natural sense of playfulness and creativity to enable the child to grow spiritually.

Lent and Easter

During the six weeks of Lent, Christians prepare for Easter by following the events of Jesus' life that led up to his death and rising to new life. *Play and Pray through Lent* encourages children and families to participate in the story in a creative way.

How to use this book

Each week there is a double-page spread comprising three distinct sections:

Getting ready

- Theme for the week
- Bible focus providing the background for the story cloth activities
- Story for the week telling the gospel story in simple language

Let's play and pray...

- Story cloth activities for each day of the week
- Talk-about ideas suggesting daily topics to talk about together
- Prayer for the week to end each day's activity and for use in addition to, or in place of, the Sunday Collect
- Song for the week. On pages 54–74 you will find suggestions for a song for each week, which may be sung at home as part of the daily activities and also incorporated into the Sunday worship. The songs are all sung to well-known nursery rhyme tunes.

Celebrating on Sunday

- Take-to-church suggestions for items to be taken to church each Sunday
- Sunday worship suggestions for how the minister or worship leader might link the project into the Sunday worship. This may take place at any appropriate point in the service and could be used as the sermon slot. The prayer for the week may be used in addition to, or in place of, the Sunday Collect.

Practical points

You will need:
- an empty shoebox
- sand-coloured cloth for the desert (70cm x 94cm)
- green cloth for the garden (70cm x 94cm)
- a space set aside at home for the story cloth activities
- a larger space in church or Junior Church
- scissors and copies of the templates on pages 76–96, cut out and stuck on to card
- felt-tipped pens to colour in each card item
- Blu-tack (for Year B only)
- sticky tape to fix tabs to back of all card items so that they will stand (see template on page 77)
- a piece of dark purple material (for Year C only)

The cloths and other items may be stored in the shoebox and laid out each day. However, if space allows, the relevant cloth should be left on display throughout the duration of the project, providing a 'special' or 'sacred' space in the home. Similarly, in church, this 'special' or 'sacred' space may be maintained throughout Lent so that anyone entering the building may witness the transformation from desert to Easter garden.

When to start

Although Ash Wednesday is the first day of Lent, in order to complete the story in the first week of Lent you will need to start *Play and Pray through Lent* on the first *Monday* of the week in which the beginning of Lent falls.

First week of Lent

Getting ready

Theme
Jesus in the desert

Bible focus
Jesus answered, 'Go away Satan! The Scriptures say: "Worship the Lord your God and serve only him."'
MATTHEW 4:10

Story for the week
One day, God's Spirit, the Holy Spirit, led Jesus into the desert. Jesus was alone in the stony desert for 40 days and had nothing to eat. After this time, the devil came to Jesus and tried to turn him away from God. The devil said to Jesus, 'If you are God's Son, tell these stones to turn into bread.' Jesus said, 'No! The Bible says that you need more than food to live.' Next, the devil took Jesus to the top of the temple in the holy city of Jerusalem. The devil said, 'Jump off! God's angels will save you.' Jesus said, 'No! The Bible says that you must not test God.' Lastly, the devil took Jesus to the top of a very high mountain, where he saw all the countries of the world. The devil said, 'Kneel down, worship me and I will make you king of all the world.' Jesus said, 'Go away, Satan! The Bible says that you must worship God and no one else.' When the devil had tried all his tricks, he went away. Then, angels came to look after Jesus.

 Let's play and pray…

Story cloth activities

Monday
Jesus is alone in the stony desert.
　Collect some stones to make a stony desert and place them on the cloth.

Tuesday
The devil says, 'If you are God's Son, tell these stones to turn into bread.'
　Cut out the figure of Jesus from the template on page 77, colour him and stand him in the middle of the stones.

Wednesday
The devil says, 'Jump off the temple! God's angels will save you.'
　Cut out a temple shape from the template on page 76 and stand it near Jesus on the cloth.

Thursday
The devil takes Jesus to a mountain top and says, 'Worship me and I will give you the world.'
　Cut out a mountain shape from the template on page 76 and stand it near Jesus on the cloth.

Friday
Jesus tells the devil to go away.
　Take away the stones, temple and mountain.

Saturday
The devil leaves Jesus and angels come to care for him.
　Cut out two angel shapes from the template on page 77 and stand them next to Jesus.

Talk about

- Monday — What might it feel like to be lonely and alone?
- Tuesday — What does it feel like when you are hungry?
- Wednesday — Talk about being dared to do something.
- Thursday — What might it feel like looking down from a mountain or hilltop?
- Friday — Talk about how hard it can be to say 'No'.
- Saturday — Talk about feeling safe and cared for.

Prayer for the week

Loving God, you sent your Holy Spirit to help Jesus when he was alone in the desert. Send your Holy Spirit to help us every day. Amen

Song for the week

Jesus sat, all alone (Tune: This old man)
See page 54.

Celebrating on Sunday

The first Sunday of Lent

Take to church

Take to church one of the stones you have collected.

Sunday worship

For the minister or worship leader

You will need:
- the desert cloth
- a bucket of extra stones for everyone in the congregation

During the service

The minister or worship leader may explore and develop the talking points, then say the prayer for the week, inviting people to bring stones to place on the cloth. The children may end this time by singing the song for the week (see page 54).

Second week of Lent

 **Getting ready**

Theme
Jesus talks about eternal life

Bible focus
God loved the people of this world so much that he gave his only Son, so that everyone who has faith in him will have eternal life and never really die.
JOHN 3:16

Story for the week
In Jerusalem, there lived a Jewish teacher. He was called Nicodemus. He saw all the things Jesus did. One dark night, Nicodemus came to see Jesus, in secret. They sat down to talk. Nicodemus told Jesus, 'I think that God helps you with all the wonderful things you do.' Jesus answered, 'You are an honest man, Nicodemus, but you must be born again before you can see God's kingdom.' Nicodemus looked puzzled. He did not know what Jesus meant. Jesus told Nicodemus what he meant. Jesus said that Nicodemus must be baptized. He must be washed clean in water to receive God's Spirit, the Holy Spirit. Jesus added, 'The Spirit of God is like the wind blowing everywhere.' Finally, Jesus told Nicodemus something very important. He said, 'God sent me to save the people of this world and to give you a new kind of life. But first, I have to die on the cross.'

 Let's play and pray...

 Story cloth activities

Monday
Nicodemus comes to talk to Jesus at night in Jerusalem.
   Cut out and colour the Jerusalem shape from the template on page 78. Stand it on the cloth and move your Jesus figure there.

Tuesday
Jesus talks about being born again.
   Place a picture of a baby or a newborn animal next to Jesus.

Wednesday
Jesus tells Nicodemus that he needs to receive God's Spirit.
   Place a feather on the cloth to represent the Spirit of God.

Thursday
Jesus says that the Holy Spirit is like the blowing wind.
   Cut out and colour the kite shape from the template on page 78 and stand it next to Jesus.

Friday
Jesus knows that he has to die on the cross.
   Cut out a cross shape from the template on page 78 and stand it beside Jesus.

Saturday
God sent Jesus to save the people of this world.
   Cut out and colour the world shape from the template on page 78 and stand it next to Jesus.

Talk about

- **Monday** Think about talking to Jesus in secret.
- **Tuesday** Talk about how exciting it is when a baby human or animal is born.
- **Wednesday** Talk about how feathers are tickly, soft, light and easy to blow away.
- **Thursday** What does it feel like, being out on a windy day?
- **Friday** Why do we have crosses and crucifixes in church?
- **Saturday** Think about how much God loves us.

Prayer for the week

Loving God, you loved the world so much that you sent Jesus. Help us to believe and trust in him, so that we may receive the new life he brings. Amen

Song for the week

We know God so loved the world (Tune: The Grand Old Duke of York)
See page 55.

Celebrating on Sunday

The second Sunday of Lent

Take to church

Take to church a picture of a baby or newborn animal.

Sunday worship

For the minister or worship leader

You will need:
- extra pictures of babies or newborn animals for everyone in the congregation

During the service

The minister or worship leader may explore and develop the talking points, then say the prayer for the week, inviting people to bring pictures of babies or newborn animals to place on the cloth. The children may end this time by singing the song for the week (see page 55).

Third week of Lent

 **Getting ready**

Theme
Jesus talks about living water

Bible focus
Jesus said, 'No one who drinks the water I give will ever be thirsty again. The water I give is like a flowing fountain that gives eternal life.'
JOHN 4:14

Story for the week
One day, Jesus was resting by a well. It was called Jacob's Well. He was hot and thirsty. A Samaritan woman came to the well to get water. Jesus asked her for a drink of water. She was shocked! Jewish people and Samaritan people were not friendly towards each other. Then Jesus said something strange: 'I can give you living water.' The woman was puzzled, as Jesus had no bucket with which to get water from the well. Jesus told her that living water was like having a water spring inside you. It gives you a new kind of life. Quietly, the woman asked, 'Sir, can I have some?'

As they talked, the woman grew more and more surprised. Jesus seemed to know all about her. She ran back into town and told everyone, 'Come and see a man who knows all about me. I wonder, has he come from God?' Many people went out to see Jesus and they believed that he was the Saviour of the world.

 Let's play and pray...

 Story cloth activities

Monday
Jesus is hot and thirsty and rests by Jacob's well.
　Cut out and colour the well from the template on page 79 and stand it on the cloth. Move Jesus to the well.

Tuesday
Jesus asks the Samaritan woman to give him a drink.
　Cut out and colour the Samaritan woman from the template on page 79 and stand her next to the well.

Wednesday
Jesus says, 'When you drink water from the well, you get thirsty again.'
　Place a small container of water next to the well.

Thursday
Jesus says, 'I can give you living water.'
　Cut out and colour the waterfall shape from the template on page 79 and stand it next to the well.

Friday
The woman says, 'Come and see a man who knows all about me.'
　Cut out and colour the crowd shape from the template on page 79 and stand it a little way from the well.

Saturday
Many people believe that Jesus is the Saviour of the world.
　Move the world shape (used last week) to the centre of the cloth and put Jesus to stand by it.

Talk about

- **Monday** What does it feel like when you are hot and thirsty?
- **Tuesday** Talk about being friendly to people.
- **Wednesday** How do you get water from a well?
- **Thursday** Talk about rushing water in springs, waterfalls and rivers.
- **Friday** Talk about any special things you have done.
- **Saturday** What do you believe about Jesus?

Prayer for the week

Loving God, you sent Jesus to be the living water. Help us to be refreshed by his living water every day. Amen

Song for the week

When you're thirsty and you know it (Tune: If you're happy and you know it)
See page 56.

Celebrating on Sunday

The third Sunday of Lent

Take to church

Take to church a small container of water.

Sunday worship

For the minister or worship leader

You will need:
- a big container for water
- small containers of water for everyone in the congregation

During the service

The minister or worship leader may explore and develop the talking points, then say the prayer for the week, inviting everyone to pour water into the big container on the cloth. The children may end this time by singing the song for the week (see page 56).

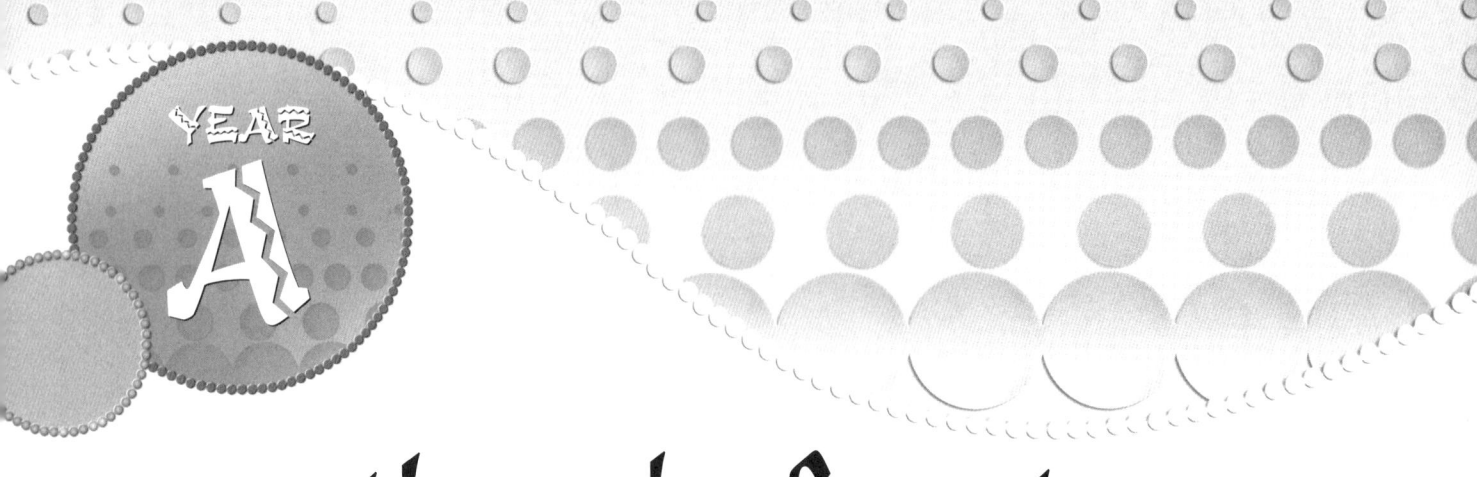

Fourth week of Lent

 Getting ready

Theme

Jesus shows the power of God

Bible focus

Jesus answered, 'Because of his blindness, you will see God perform a miracle for him.'
JOHN 9:3

Story for the week

One day, as Jesus was walking along, he saw a man who was blind. The man had been blind since he was born. Jesus said to the people around him, 'While I am in the world, I am the light for the world.' Then Jesus did something strange: he spat on the ground and made some mud, which he put over the man's eyes. Then he sent the man to Siloam Pool to wash the mud off. The man did as Jesus had said. He went to Siloam Pool, knelt down at the side and washed his face. When he had washed the mud off, he could see! His neighbours were amazed and asked what had happened. He told them about Jesus.

The Pharisees asked the man about his healing. He told them, 'Jesus is sent from God and he has made me see.' This made the Pharisees very angry. Later, Jesus went to find the man and told him that many people did not know about him—they were still in the dark. The healed man believed in Jesus.

Let's play and pray...

Story cloth activities

Monday

Jesus meets the blind man.

Cut out and colour the shape of the blind man from the template on page 80 and stand him with Jesus on the cloth.

Tuesday

Jesus says, 'I am the light for the world.'

Place a nightlight on the world next to Jesus.

Wednesday

Jesus covers the blind man's eyes with mud.

Find a small piece of mud and place it next to Jesus.

Thursday

Jesus sends the blind man to the Pool of Siloam.

Cut out a piece of foil to make a pool, place it on the cloth and move the blind man next to it.

Friday

The Pharisees ask the man how he had been healed.

Cut out the shape of a question mark from the template on page 80 and stand it next to the blind man.

Saturday

Jesus says that many people are still in the dark about him.

Cut out and colour a pair of dark glasses from the template on page 80 and stand it near Jesus.

Talk about

- **Monday** What might it feel like to be blind?
- **Tuesday** Why did Jesus say that he was 'the light for the world'?
- **Wednesday** Talk about old-fashioned and modern-day cures for illness.
- **Thursday** Talk about people visiting holy wells and spas.
- **Friday** Questions—why do we ask them?
- **Saturday** Talk about people who are still 'blind' to Jesus and do not believe in him.

Prayer for the week

Loving God, you sent your son Jesus to show us your power. Bring the power of your love into our lives every day. Amen

Song for the week

Jesus met a blind man sitting by the road (Tune: She'll be coming round the mountain)
See page 57.

Fourth week of Lent

Tune: She'll be coming round the mountain

Jesus met a blind man sitting by the road.
Jesus met a blind man sitting by the road.
Jesus met a blind man sitting, met a blind man sitting,
Met a blind man sitting by the road.

Jesus cured him with some spit and some mud.
Jesus cured him with some spit and some mud.
Jesus cured him with some spit, cured him with some spit,
Cured him with some spit and some mud.

And now he can see the Son of God.
And now he can see the Son of God.
With his eyes wide open, eyes wide open,
Now he can see the Son of God.

Celebrating on Sunday

The fourth Sunday of Lent (Mothering Sunday)

Take to church

Take a nightlight to church.

Sunday worship

For the minister or worship leader

> **You will need:**
> - extra nightlights for everyone in the congregation

During the service

The minister or worship leader may explore and develop the talking points, then say the prayer for the week, inviting people to bring nightlights to place on the cloth. The children may end this time by singing the song for the week (see page 57).

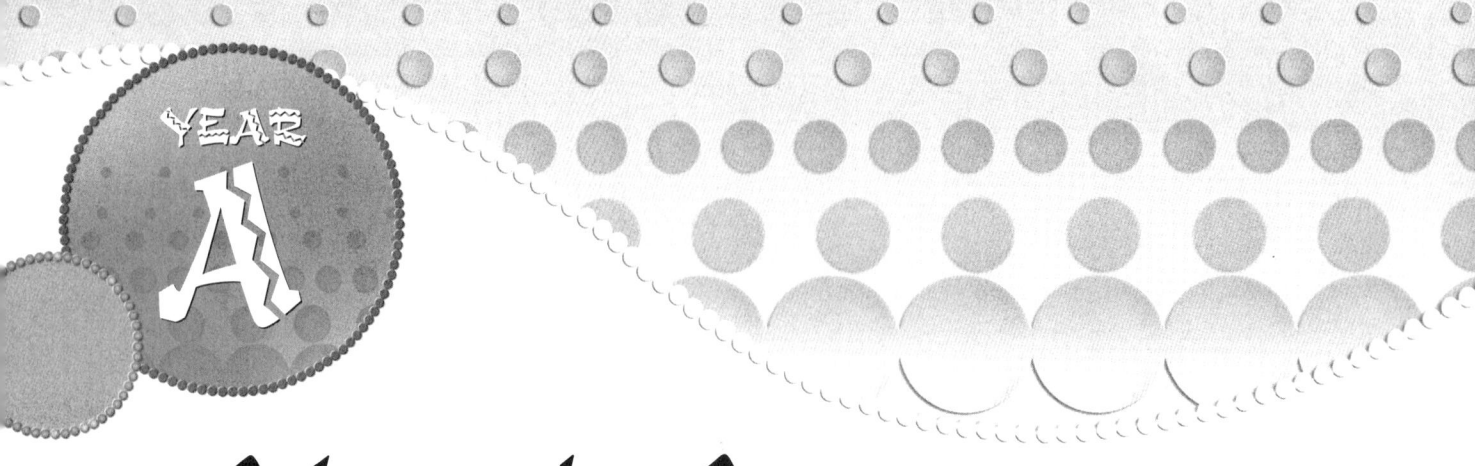

Fifth week of Lent

 ## Getting ready

Theme
Jesus brings new life from death

Bible focus
Jesus then said, 'I am the one who raises the dead to life! Everyone who has faith in me will live, even if they die.'
JOHN 11:25

Story for the week
One day, Jesus had a message from his friends Mary and Martha. Their brother Lazarus was very ill. They asked Jesus to come to Bethany to visit Lazarus. Now, Jesus loved Lazarus and knew he might die. But Jesus decided to stay on in Jerusalem for two more days. By the time Jesus eventually got to Bethany, Lazarus had already died and had been buried in a tomb for four days. Martha and Mary were very upset. They told Jesus, 'If you had been here, our brother would not have died.' Jesus said, 'Your brother will live again.' Jesus was terribly upset seeing Mary crying. Jesus also cried. He went to the tomb. It was a cave with a stone rolled against the entrance. Jesus told the people to roll away the stone. Then he looked up to heaven and prayed. Then he shouted, 'Lazarus, come out!' and Lazarus came out. Jesus told the people to untie Lazarus's bandages. Lazarus was alive.

 ## Let's play and pray...

 ### Story cloth activities

Monday
Jesus hears that his friend is ill in Bethany.
  Cut out and colour the Bethany signpost from the template on page 81. Stand Jesus and his disciples (see template on page 83) next to it.

Tuesday
Jesus tells his disciples that Lazarus will die.
  Cut out and colour the tomb and stone shapes from the template on page 82. Put the stone over the entrance. Stand it near the edge of the cloth.

Wednesday
Jesus tells Martha and Mary that Lazarus will live again.
  Cut out the Mary and Martha shapes from the template on page 81 and stand them and Jesus near the tomb.

Thursday
Jesus cries.
  Place a handkerchief or tissue next to Jesus.

Friday
Jesus prays and calls Lazarus out of the tomb.
  Take away the stone from the entrance of the tomb and move the crowd shape (from the template on page 81) next to it.

Saturday

Lazarus walks out of the tomb and the people take off his bandages.

Place a small strip of white cloth or bandage near the tomb. Place the green (garden) cloth next to the desert cloth.

Talk about

Monday How do we feel when someone we know is very ill?

Tuesday How do we feel when we hear that someone we know has died?

Wednesday How did Mary and Martha feel when Jesus said that Lazarus would live again?

Thursday Talk about the times when we cry—sad times and happy times.

Friday Talk about Jesus praying in front of the tomb. What do we pray to God about?

Saturday How did Mary and Martha feel when they saw that Lazarus was alive?

Prayer for the week

Loving God, Jesus gave new life to Lazarus, when he was buried in the tomb. Give us new life too. Amen

Song for the week

Lazarus was very ill
(Tune: Old MacDonald)
See page 58.

Celebrating on Sunday

The fifth Sunday of Lent

Take to church

Take a strip of white cloth or bandage to church.

Sunday worship

For the minister or worship leader

You will need:
- strips of white cloth or bandage for everyone in the congregation

During the service

The minister or worship leader may explore and develop the talking points, then say the prayer for the week, inviting people to bring strips of white cloth or bandages to place on the cloth. The children may end this time by singing the song for the week (see page 58).

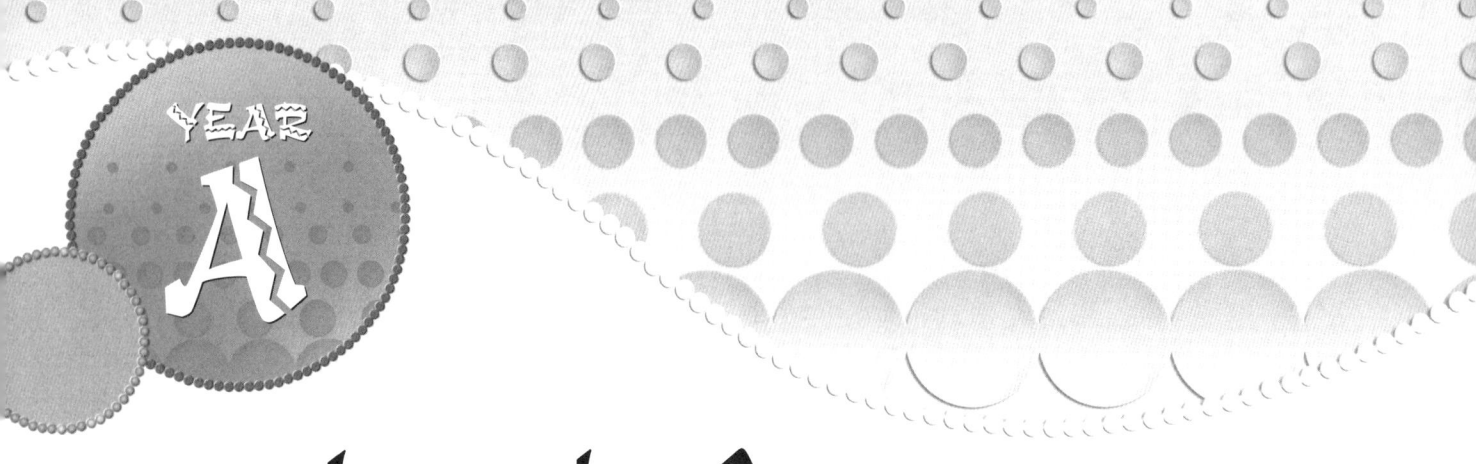

Sixth week of Lent

 **Getting ready**

Theme
Jesus shares the last supper with his friends

Bible focus
During the meal Jesus took some bread in his hands. He blessed the bread and broke it. Then he gave it to his disciples and said, 'Take this and eat it. This is my body.'
MATTHEW 26:26

Story for the week
The religious leaders were Jesus' enemies. Judas went to them, in secret, and said, 'I will help you arrest Jesus.' They were very pleased and paid Judas 30 silver coins. After that, Judas made his plans to betray Jesus. On Thursday evening, Jesus and his disciples met in an upper room for the Passover meal. Jesus seemed very sad. As they ate, Jesus talked of many things. Then he said, 'One of you will betray me.' The disciples were all very upset to hear these words. Judas quietly left the room. When they had eaten, Jesus took a loaf of bread. He thanked God for it, broke it, and shared the bread with his disciples. 'Take this and eat it. This is my body,' he said. Then, Jesus took a cup of wine, thanked God for it, and gave it to his disciples. 'Take this and drink it. This is my blood,' he said. Jesus told them that he was going to die, but no one wanted to believe him.

 Let's play and pray...

 Story cloth activities

Monday
Judas plans to betray Jesus.
   Move Jesus on to the green cloth. Cut out and colour Judas from the template on page 83 and stand him, with some coins, near to Jesus.

Tuesday
Jesus and the disciples have the Passover meal together.
   Cut out and colour the plate of Passover food from the template on page 83 and stand it near to Jesus.

Wednesday
Jesus says that one of the disciples will betray him.
   Stand the disciples next to Jesus. Move Judas and the coins far away from Jesus.

Thursday
Jesus takes bread and breaks it.
   Place a small piece of bread next to the Passover plate.

Friday
Jesus takes a cup of wine, gives thanks and offers it to the disciples.
   Make a wine glass out of foil and place it next to the Passover plate.

Saturday
Jesus must die.
   Move the cross shape and stand it on the cloth behind Jesus.

Talk about

Monday — Talk about being loyal to friends.
Tuesday — How might Jesus have felt, eating this last meal with his friends?
Wednesday — How does it feel to be betrayed or let down by your friends?
Thursday — Talk about eating bread and the special bread we have in church.
Friday — Talk about wine and the special wine we have in church.
Saturday — Talk about how Jesus might have felt, knowing he had to die on the cross.

 Prayer for the week

Loving God, Jesus was betrayed by one of his disciples. Help us to be Jesus' friends, to follow him and never let him down. Amen

Song for the week

Take, eat, this bread, it is my body (Tune: Baa Baa Black Sheep)
See page 59.

 Celebrating on Sunday

The sixth Sunday of Lent (Palm Sunday)

Take to church

Take a coin to church.

Sunday worship

For the minister or worship leader

You will need:
- extra coins for everyone in the congregation

During the service

The minister or worship leader may explore and develop the talking points, then say the prayer for the week, inviting people to bring coins to place on the cloth. The children may end this time by singing the song for the week (see page 59).

Holy Week

Getting ready

Theme
Jesus is alive

Bible focus
Then Jesus said, 'Don't be afraid! Tell my followers to go to Galilee. They will see me there.'
MATTHEW 28:10

Story for the week

Jesus' enemies had captured him after the last meal with his disciples. Jesus had died on the cross on the Friday and was buried in a tomb with a huge stone over the front, covering the entrance. It was now very early on Sunday morning, just before the sun came up. Two women, Mary Magdalene and another Mary, were walking to the tomb. They carried spices and ointments. Suddenly, the ground shook with a strong earthquake. A shining white angel rolled away the stone from the tomb and sat on it. The soldiers guarding the tomb were so scared that they fell down as if they were dead. The women were scared too. The angel said to them, 'Don't be afraid! Jesus isn't here. He is alive. Hurry! Go and tell his disciples that Jesus is alive.'

The women started to run off. Suddenly, Jesus was standing there. They knelt down in front of him, holding on to his feet. Jesus told them not to be afraid but to tell his friends that he would see them in Galilee.

Let's play and pray...

Story cloth activities

Monday
Jesus dies on the cross and is buried in the tomb.
Put the Jesus figure in the box. Move the tomb shape on to the green cloth, with the stone in front.

Tuesday
Mary Magdalene and the other Mary come to see the tomb, bringing spices.
Cut out and colour the two Marys from the template on page 84 and stand them on the way to the tomb. *(Salome is also needed in Year B.)*

Wednesday
There is an earthquake and a shining white angel rolls back the stone.
Roll back the stone. Take one of your angel shapes, spread glitter on it and stand it near the tomb.

Thursday
An angel tells the women that Jesus has risen.
Move the two Marys next to the angel.

Friday
The women see Jesus in the garden. He is alive!
Stand Jesus in front of the two Marys. Take the cross, decorate it with flowers and stand it behind the tomb.

Saturday

Jesus says, 'Tell my friends that I will see them in Galilee.'

Cut out and colour the word Galilee from the template on page 84 and stand it on the edge of the green (garden) cloth.

Talk about

Monday What can we do to remember people who have died?
Tuesday How did the two Marys feel as they walked to the tomb?
Wednesday Talk about what happens in an earthquake.
Thursday Talk about other Bible stories of angels who brought messages.
Friday How did the women feel when they saw that Jesus was alive?
Saturday Talk about visiting favourite places.

 **Prayer for the week**

Loving God, your Son Jesus suffered pain and injustice. He died and has risen to life again. Help us to know that Jesus is alive and always with us. Amen

Song for the week

Let us go to the tomb (Tune: Happy birthday to you)
See page 60.

 ## Celebrating on Sunday

Easter Day

Take to church

Take a flower to church.

Sunday worship

For the minister or worship leader

You will need:
- extra flowers for everyone in the congregation
- a container to hold the flowers

During the service

The minister or worship leader may explore and develop the talking points, then say the prayer for the week, inviting people to bring their flowers to place in the container on the cloth. The children may end this time by singing the song for the week (see page 60).

First week of Lent

 Getting ready

Theme

Jesus in the desert

Bible focus

Straight away God's Spirit made Jesus go into the desert. He stayed there for forty days while Satan tested him. Jesus was with the wild animals, but angels took care of him.

MARK 1:12–13

Story for the week

One day, Jesus left his home at Nazareth in Galilee and went down to the River Jordan. He saw a crowd of people down by the river. Jesus went down to see. John the Baptist was baptizing people in the water as a sign that they were sorry for the things they had done wrong. Jesus asked John, 'Will you baptize me too?' So Jesus went down into the water. As Jesus came up out of the water, he saw the sky open and the Holy Spirit came down to him like a dove. Then Jesus heard God's voice from heaven saying, 'You are my own dear Son and I am pleased with you.'

After that, God's Spirit, the Holy Spirit, made Jesus go into the stony desert. Jesus was alone in the desert for 40 days and 40 nights. Jesus went into the desert to prepare for the work that God wanted him to do. Satan, the devil, came and tried to make Jesus to turn away from God, but Jesus refused to be tempted. Then angels came to care for Jesus.

 Let's play and pray…

 Story cloth activities

Monday
Jesus is baptized in the River Jordan.
  Make a river out of foil, shiny material or blue wool and place it on the cloth.

Tuesday
The Holy Spirit comes down to Jesus like a dove.
  Cut out and colour Jesus and the dove from the templates on pages 77 and 85 and stand them by the river.

Wednesday
God's Spirit made Jesus go into the desert.
  Collect stones to make a stony desert and place them on the cloth. Place Jesus with the stones.

Thursday
Jesus is in the desert for 40 days with the wild animals.
  Cut out and colour some wild animal shapes from the template on page 85 or find model animals to stand on the cloth, near the stones.

Friday
Jesus is tempted by the devil.
  Place some favourite sweets near Jesus, but resist the temptation to eat them.

Saturday
Angels take care of Jesus.
  Draw a picture of someone who cares for you and place it with Jesus on the cloth.

Talk about

Monday Talk about bath time and feeling clean. Talk about how water is used to symbolize cleanliness in baptism.

Tuesday Talk about the dove as a symbol of the Holy Spirit. Talk about how God gives us his Holy Spirit when we are baptized.

Wednesday What might it be like to be in the desert?

Thursday Talk about wild animals you know about, and endangered species.

Friday What does it feel like to be tempted?

Saturday Think about all the people who care for us and help us.

Prayer for the week

Loving God, your Holy Spirit was with Jesus when he was tempted in the desert. Send your Holy Spirit to help us every day. Amen

Song for the week

Jesus needed time alone (Tune: The animals marched in two by two, hurrah, hurrah)

See page 61.

Year B

First week of Lent

Tune: The animals marched in two by two, hurrah, hurrah!

Jesus needed time alone—to pray, to pray.
Jesus needed time alone—to pray, to pray.
Jesus needed time to pray
So all alone he went away,
And God's angels came to take great care of him.

Jesus prayed for forty days—to God, to God.
Jesus prayed for forty days—to God, to God.
Jesus prayed for forty days
In the desert where he stayed,
And God's angels came to take great care of him.

Satan tempted God's own Son—O dear, O dear.
Satan tempted God's own Son—O dear, O dear.
Satan tempted God's own Son,
He tried and tried, but Jesus won,
And God's angels came to take great care of him.

The angels came to bring him food—hurrah, hurrah.
The angels came to bring him food—hurrah, hurrah.
The angels came to bring him food,
For Jesus is the Son of God,
Yes, God's angels came to take great care of him.

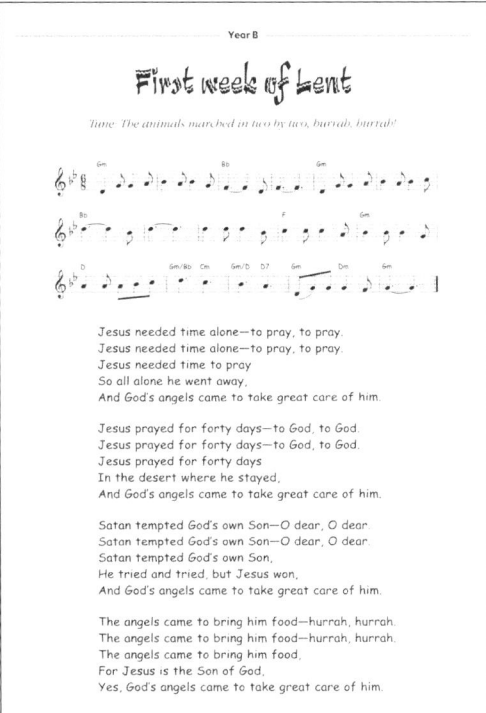

Celebrating on Sunday

The first Sunday of Lent

Take to church

Take one of the stones you have collected to church.

Sunday worship

For the minister or worship leader

You will need:

- the desert cloth
- material to represent the river
- a bucket of extra stones for everyone in the congregation

During the service

The minister or worship leader may explore and develop the talking points, then say the prayer for the week, inviting people to bring stones to place on the cloth. The children may end this time by singing the song for the week (see page 61).

Second week of Lent

 Getting ready

Theme

Jesus invites people to follow him

Bible focus

Jesus then told the crowd and the disciples to come closer, and he said: If any of you want to be my followers, you must forget about yourself. You must take up your cross and follow me.

MARK 8:34

Story for the week

One day Jesus and his disciples were walking along the road to Jerusalem. He told them, 'When I go to Jerusalem, the religious leaders and other people will reject me. I will suffer and die but three days later I will be alive again.' The disciples were all very upset by what Jesus said. Peter took Jesus aside and told him not to say things like that. Jesus turned and looked at all the disciples. Then he said to Peter, 'Get away from me. You are like Satan! You are thinking like everyone else and not like God.' Then Jesus called everyone to come closer. He told them to listen carefully. Then he said, 'If you want to come with me and be my followers, you must forget about yourselves. You must put aside all your own needs and wants. You must take up your cross and follow me.'

 Let's play and pray...

 Story cloth activities

Monday
Jesus and his disciples are on the way to Jerusalem.
  Place a strip of material on the cloth to represent the road to Jerusalem. Stand Jesus on the road.

Tuesday
Jesus tells the disciples that the people will reject him.
  Cut out and colour the disciples from the template on page 83 and stand them on the road, just behind Jesus.

Wednesday
Peter tries to argue with Jesus.
  Draw a picture of someone you have argued with and place it near Jesus.

Thursday
Jesus says that those who want to come with him must forget about themselves.
  Share the sweets you placed in the desert with someone else.

Friday
Jesus says that those who want to come with him must carry their own cross.
  Cut out a cross from the template on page 78 and stand it between Jesus and the disciples.

Saturday
Jesus invites people to follow him.
  Draw round your feet, cut out and colour the shapes and place them on the road behind Jesus.

Talk about

- Monday — Talk about travelling on roads and journeys.
- Tuesday — What does it feel like when people are friendly to you?
- Wednesday — Talk about someone you have argued with and how you felt.
- Thursday — How do you feel about sharing?
- Friday — Talk about things that make following Jesus difficult.
- Saturday — What does it mean to follow Jesus?

Prayer for the week

Loving God, your Son Jesus invited people to walk in his footsteps. Help us to follow Jesus more closely each day. Amen

Song for the week

Jesus is going to Jerusalem (Tune: Ten green bottles)
See page 62.

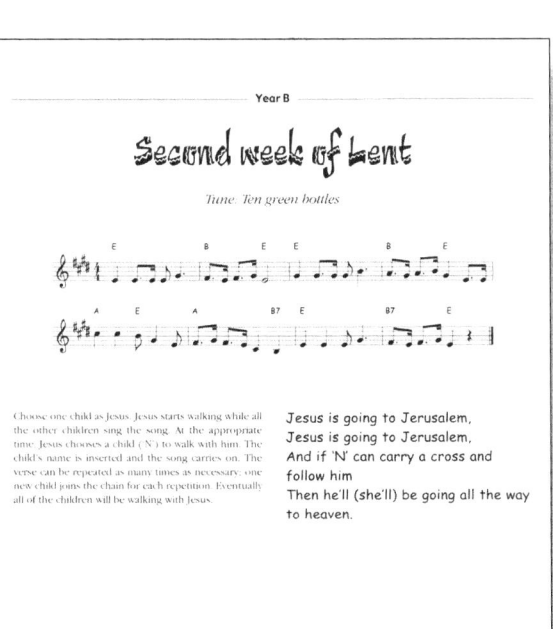

Celebrating on Sunday

The second Sunday of Lent

Take to church

Take one of the footprints you made to church.

Sunday worship

For the minister or worship leader

You will need:
- a strip of material for the road
- extra footprints for everyone in the congregation

During the service

The minister or worship leader may explore and develop the talking points, then say the prayer for the week, inviting people to bring footprints to place on the road. The children may end this time by singing the song for the week (see page 62).

Third week of Lent

 **Getting ready**

Theme
Jesus clears the temple

Bible focus
Jesus said to the people who had been selling doves, 'Get those doves out of here! Don't make my Father's house a market place.'
JOHN 2:16

Story for the week
One day, Jesus and his disciples went up to Jerusalem for the Passover festival. They climbed up the hill to the big temple. The temple was as noisy as the market place. It was full of people selling cattle, sheep and doves for the sacrifices. Jesus saw the money changers sitting at their tables. People were going to the tables to change their money for the special temple coins. Jesus saw how the money changers cheated people. Jesus felt very angry that all this was happening in the temple. Jesus took some rope and made a whip. Then he used his whip to chase all the people out of the temple, together with the sheep and the cattle. Next, he turned over the tables of the money changers, scattering their coins all over the floor. Then, Jesus said to the people who had been selling doves, 'Get those doves out of here! Don't make my Father's house a market place.'

 Let's play and pray...

 Story cloth activities

Monday
Jesus goes up to Jerusalem for the Passover.
 Cut out and colour the city of Jerusalem from the template on page 78, or use wooden blocks to make the city of Jerusalem on the cloth.

Tuesday
Jesus goes into the temple.
 Cut out and colour the temple shape from the template on page 76 and stand it beside the city of Jerusalem. Stand Jesus in front of the temple.

Wednesday
Jesus sees people selling cattle, sheep and doves.
 Cut out and colour dove, cattle and sheep shapes from the templates on pages 85 and 86 and stand them in front of the temple.

Thursday
Jesus sees the money changers.
 Place some small coins next to the animals in front of the temple.

Friday
Jesus is angry and makes a whip out of cords.
 Place a shoelace or piece of string near the figure of Jesus.

Saturday
Jesus says, 'Take these things away.'
 Remove all the animals, coins and whip from the temple.

Talk about

Monday Talk about visiting towns and cities.

Tuesday Talk about going into your church or a large cathedral.

Wednesday Talk about visiting the stalls in your local market. What can you buy there?

Thursday Talk about going to the bank for money.

Friday What does it feel like when you are angry?

Saturday Talk about cleaning and clearing up your room.

Prayer for the week

Loving God, your Son Jesus made the temple clean. Help us to clear away the wrong things we say and do. Amen

Song for the week

My Father's house is a house of prayer (Tune: The wheels on the bus)

See page 63.

My Father's house is a house of prayer,
House of prayer,
House of prayer.
My Father's house is a house of prayer
All day long.

You have made it a den of thieves,
Den of thieves,
Den of thieves.
You have made it a den of thieves
All day long.

Tip the tables, spill the coins,
Spill the coins,
Spill the coins.
Tip the tables, spill the coins
All day long.

Now it's quiet, we can pray,
We can pray,
We can pray.
Now it's quiet, we can pray
All day long.

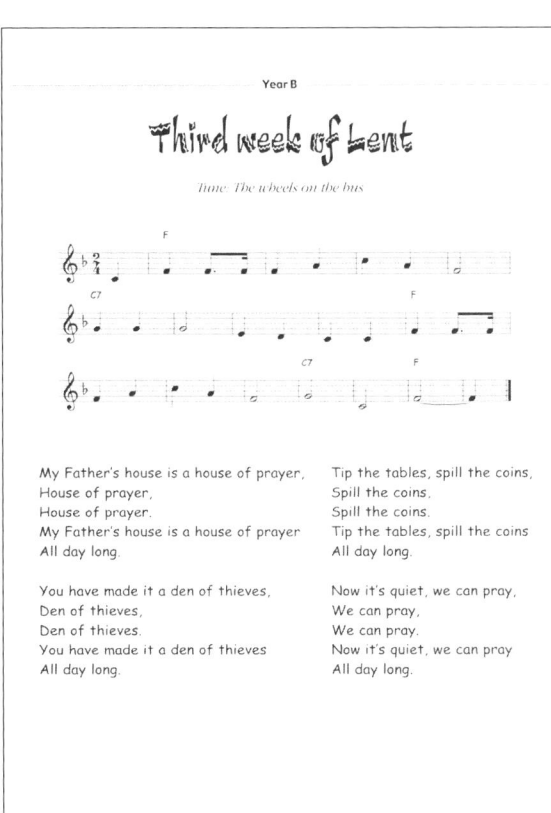

Celebrating on Sunday

The third Sunday of Lent

Take to church

Take a 'city of Jerusalem' shape, or some of the wooden blocks representing the city of Jerusalem, to church.

Sunday worship

For the minister or worship leader

You will need:

- the temple
- a box of 'city of Jerusalem' shapes for everyone in the congregation, or wooden blocks

During the service

The minister or worship leader may explore and develop the talking points, then say the prayer for the week, inviting people to bring the city of Jerusalem to place on the cloth. The children may end this time by singing the song for the week (see page 63).

Fourth week of Lent

 Getting ready

Theme
Jesus, the way to life

Bible focus
Then everyone who has faith in the Son of Man will have eternal life.
JOHN 3:15

Story for the week
One day, Jesus was talking to his friend Nicodemus. He told Nicodemus that a long time ago God had given Moses a special sign. This sign was a snake made out of metal. When Moses and the people of God were crossing the desert, many people got bitten by poisonous snakes. When Moses lifted up the metal snake so that people could see it, they were cured from their snakebites. Jesus said that God wants him to be our sign and that, one day, he would be lifted up on the cross. We can follow Jesus and he will show us the right way to live. God loves us so much that he sent Jesus into the world to tell us that we can all have a new kind of life if we believe in him. Jesus is like a great light shining into the dark world to help us to see clearly. Jesus came to show us how to choose the right way to live and how to please God.

 **Let's play and pray...**

 Story cloth activities

Monday
Jesus asks us to choose the right way.
   Place a strip of material to make a fork in your road.

Tuesday
Jesus knows that some roads go nowhere.
   Cut out and colour a 'No through road' sign from the template on page 87 and stand it at the side of your new road.

Wednesday
Jesus warns us of the dangerous road.
   Place stones along the new road and block the exit end.

Thursday
Jesus shows us the right way.
   Move Jesus further along the right road.

Friday
Jesus wants us to follow him.
   Move your footprints along the road behind Jesus.

Saturday
Jesus is going to the cross.
   Move the cross in front of Jesus on the road.

30

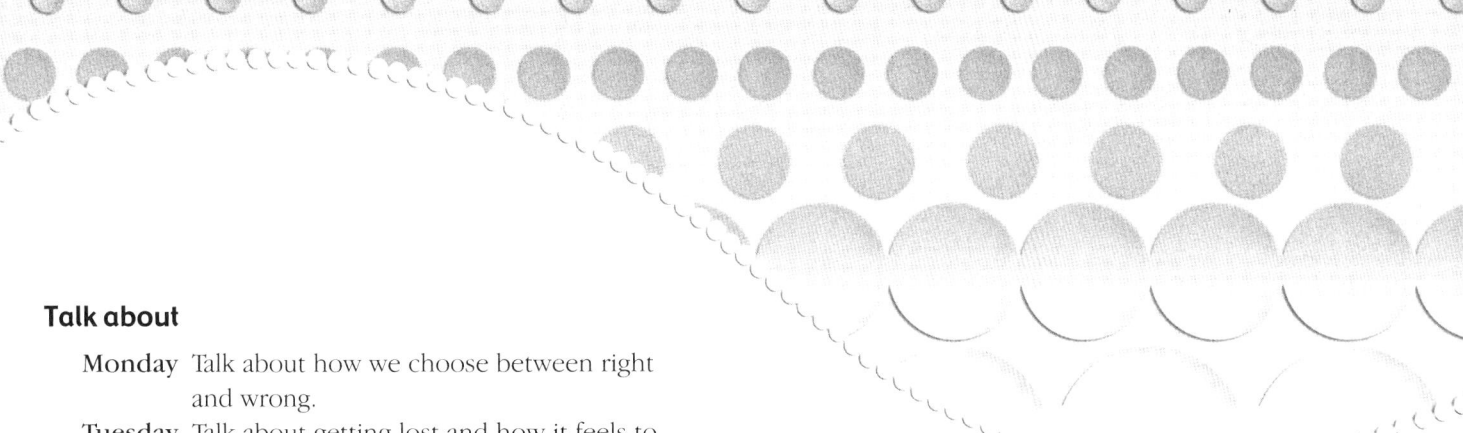

Talk about

- Monday   Talk about how we choose between right and wrong.
- Tuesday   Talk about getting lost and how it feels to be lost.
- Wednesday   Talk about feeling safe.
- Thursday   Talk about maps and things that help us find our way.
- Friday   Talk about friends and how Jesus wants to be our friend.
- Saturday   Talk about things you find difficult.

Prayer for the week

Loving God, your Son Jesus shows us the path to life. Help us to choose the road that leads to you. Amen

Song for the week

We have to make a choice (Tune: The farmer's in his den)
See page 64.

Celebrating on Sunday

The fourth Sunday of Lent (Mothering Sunday)

Take to church

Take the 'no through road' sign to church.

Sunday worship

For the minister or worship leader

You will need:
- a piece of cloth to make a fork in the road
- a box of 'no through road' signs for everyone in the congregation

During the service

The minister or worship leader may explore and develop the talking points, then say the prayer for the week, inviting people to bring the 'no through road' signs to place on the cloth. The children may end this time by singing the song for the week (see page 64).

Fifth week of Lent

 ## Getting ready

 ## Let's play and pray...

Theme
Jesus talks about his death

Bible focus
'If I am lifted up above the earth, I will make everyone want to come to me.'
JOHN 12:32

Story for the week
One day, Jesus and his disciples were in Jerusalem. It was the time of the Passover festival. Jesus knew that he was going to die soon. He told his disciples a story about plants and seeds to help them understand what was going happen to him. The wheat plant grows and makes seeds, called grain. When the grain is ripe, it falls to the ground. The plant dies, and the grain produces another wheat plant with lots more grain. But first the grain has to fall to the ground and be buried. If it is buried in the ground, it will make lots of wheat. Jesus knew that he would have to die on the cross, be buried in the ground and rise to new life, so that he could make it possible for many people to have new life with God.

When Jesus had finished telling this story, a voice came down from heaven. The people thought it was thunder but it was God's voice. God wanted people to understand what Jesus had to do. Jesus would have to die. He would be lifted up to give people new life and many people would want to follow him.

 Story cloth activities

Monday
Jesus talks about a seed.
Buy a packet of cress seeds and place the packet on the cloth.

Tuesday
Jesus says that the seed must die.
Sow half the seeds into two containers on beds of moist cottonwool. Place the packet of remaining seeds on the cloth.

Wednesday
Jesus says that the seed will make a plant with many seeds.
Place the green cloth next to the desert cloth and move the containers of growing seeds on to the green cloth.

Thursday
Jesus talks about the cross.
Move the cross on to the green cloth.

Friday
Jesus says he will be lifted up on the cross.
Move Jesus on to the green cloth and stand him next to the cross.

Saturday
Jesus says that people will follow him.
Move the disciples near to Jesus.

Talk about

- **Monday** What does a seed need to grow (water, nutrients, light and so on)?
- **Tuesday** Talk about how the seed casts off its cover to grow.
- **Wednesday** Talk about the food you eat and where it comes from.
- **Thursday** Talk about what the cross was made of—its weight and shape.
- **Friday** Talk about how Jesus felt, knowing that he would die on the cross.
- **Saturday** Talk about all the different people who believe in Jesus today.

> ### Prayer for the week
> *Loving God, your Son Jesus died to bring new life to the world. Help us to share his risen life. Amen*

Song for the week

One small seed (Tune: Three blind mice)
See page 65.

 ## Celebrating on Sunday

The fifth Sunday of Lent

Take to church

Take one of the containers of growing cress seeds to church.

Sunday worship

For the minister or worship leader

> **You will need:**
> - the sand-coloured cloth with the green cloth laid on top, covering half of it
> - extra containers with cress seeds on moist cottonwool for everyone in the congregation

During the service

The minister or worship leader may explore and develop the talking points, then say the prayer for the week, inviting people to bring the growing cress seeds to place on the green cloth. The children may end this time by singing the song for the week (see page 65).

Sixth week of Lent

 **Getting ready**

Theme
Jesus rides into Jerusalem

Bible focus
In front of Jesus and behind him, people went along shouting, 'Hooray! God bless the one who comes in the name of the Lord!'
MARK 11:9

Story for the week
Jesus was almost in Jerusalem. Jesus asked two of his disciples to go into the nearby village and bring him a young donkey. They would find the donkey tied up there. They brought the young donkey and threw their cloaks over its back for Jesus to ride on it. The people were eagerly waiting in Jerusalem. They knew Jesus was coming. They expected him to do wonderful things. Suddenly, there were some shouts and cheers. Jesus was coming up the hill to Jerusalem and he was riding on a donkey. His disciples walked with him. Jesus rode through the gates into the city. People began to wave palm branches that they had cut from the fields. Others spread palm branches to make a carpet on the road before him. Many people even spread their cloaks on the ground. The excited people crowded around Jesus and followed him along the road. They shouted out, 'Hosanna!' and 'Praise Jesus! God bless the one who comes in the name of the Lord!' It was a day they would never forget.

 Let's play and pray...

 Story cloth activities

Monday
Jesus and the disciples are almost in Jerusalem.
　Extend the road on to the green cloth and move the city of Jerusalem to the end of the road.

Tuesday
Jesus says, 'Untie the donkey and bring it here.'
　Cut out and colour a donkey shape from the template on page 88, or place a model donkey on the road.

Wednesday
The disciples bring the donkey to Jesus and throw their cloaks over it.
　Make a cloak shape out of a scrap of material and put it on the donkey.

Thursday
Many people spread their cloaks on the road.
　Cut out some more cloak shapes from scraps of material and spread them on the road.

Friday
Other people spread branches that they have cut from the field.
　Make some palm branches from the template on page 88 and spread them on the road.

Saturday
The people shout, 'Hosanna' and 'Praise Jesus'.
　Write words of praise on the palm branches.

Talk about

Monday — Talk about Jerusalem as a special place—the hill leading up to the city, the walls and the gates.
Tuesday — Talk about donkeys as working animals.
Wednesday — Talk about why important people wear special clothes, like royal robes.
Thursday — Talk about how we welcome important people.
Friday — Talk about the palm crosses you will receive on Sunday.
Saturday — What words do you use when you are glad about something?

Prayer for the week

Loving God, as your Son Jesus rode into Jerusalem, the people praised your name. Help us to praise you every day. Amen

Song for the week

Jesus came to town (Tune: One man went to mow)
See page 66.

 ## Celebrating on Sunday

The sixth Sunday of Lent (Palm Sunday)

Take to church

Take one of the cloak shapes you have made to church.

Sunday worship

For the minister or worship leader

> **You will need:**
> - a box of extra cloak shapes or small branches for everyone in the congregation

During the service

The minister or worship leader may explore and develop the talking points, then say the prayer for the week, inviting people to place the cloak shapes or small branches on the cloth. The children may end this time by singing the song for the week (see page 66).

35

Holy Week

Getting ready

Theme

Jesus is alive

Bible focus

'You are looking for Jesus from Nazareth, who was nailed to a cross. God has raised him to life, and he isn't here.'
MARK 16:6

Story for the week

When Jesus came to Jerusalem, his enemies captured him. He was put to death on a cross and buried in a stone tomb on Friday. It was now very early on Sunday morning, and it was still dark. Three women were walking sadly to the stone tomb. They were Mary Magdalene, Salome and Mary the mother of James. They were bringing spices to anoint Jesus' body. On the way, they wondered how they would roll the huge stone away from the entrance. What a surprise they had when they got there! The stone had been moved away. They went into the tomb. Sitting on the right-hand side, they saw a young man in a white robe. They were really scared! The young man said, 'Don't be afraid! You are looking for Jesus. He is alive. He isn't here. See the place where they put his body. Go and tell his disciples, and especially Peter, that he will see you in Galilee.' The women were amazed!

Let's play and pray…

Story cloth activities

Monday
Jesus dies on the cross.
  Fasten Jesus to the cross with Blu-tack.

Tuesday
Jesus is placed in the stone tomb.
  Remove Jesus. Cut out and colour the tomb and stone shapes from the templates on page 82. Stand them on the cloth, the stone covering the entrance.

Wednesday
The three women walk to the tomb, bringing spices.
  Cut out and colour three women (two Marys and Salome) from the template on page 84 and stand them on the cloth. Sprinkle perfume on cottonwool and place near the women.

Thursday
The women see that the stone has been moved.
  Move the stone and place the women and perfumed cottonwool in front of the tomb.

Friday
The young man tells the women, 'Jesus is not here.'
  Cut out a white-robed figure from the template on page 89 and stand it by the tomb.

Saturday
Jesus is alive!
  Place Jesus in the centre of the green (garden) cloth, surrounded by all the figures. Cut out and colour some flowers from the template on page 89.

Talk about

- **Monday** Talk about someone (or a pet) you have known who has died.
- **Tuesday** Talk about churchyards as peaceful places.
- **Wednesday** Talk about saying goodbye to people we love.
- **Thursday** Talk about different kinds of surprises.
- **Friday** Talk about people who bring messages.
- **Saturday** Talk about parties and celebrations for special people.

Prayer for the week

Loving God, your Son Jesus died on the cross, was buried and rose again. Help us to know that Jesus is always with us. Amen

Song for the week

Thank you, God, for Easter Day (Tune: Here we go round the mulberry bush)
See page 67.

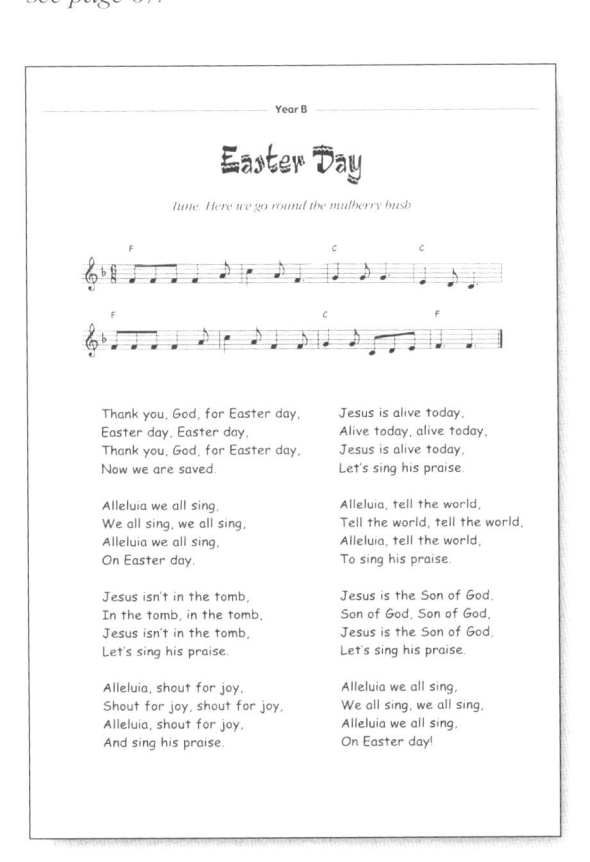

Celebrating on Sunday

Easter Day

Take to church

Take some of the flowers you have made, or some spring flowers, to church.

Sunday worship

For the minister or worship leader

You will need:
- extra flowers for everyone in the congregation

During the service

The minister or worship leader may explore and develop the talking points, then say the prayer for the week, inviting people to place flowers around the green (garden) cloth. The children may end this time by singing the song for the week (see page 67).

Year B

Easter Day

Tune: Here we go round the mulberry bush

Thank you, God, for Easter day,
Easter day, Easter day,
Thank you, God, for Easter day,
Now we are saved.

Alleluia we all sing,
We all sing, we all sing,
Alleluia we all sing,
On Easter day.

Jesus isn't in the tomb,
In the tomb, in the tomb,
Jesus isn't in the tomb,
Let's sing his praise.

Alleluia, shout for joy,
Shout for joy, shout for joy,
Alleluia, shout for joy,
And sing his praise.

Jesus is alive today,
Alive today, alive today,
Jesus is alive today,
Let's sing his praise.

Alleluia, tell the world,
Tell the world, tell the world,
Alleluia, tell the world,
To sing his praise.

Jesus is the Son of God,
Son of God, Son of God,
Jesus is the Son of God,
Let's sing his praise.

Alleluia we all sing,
We all sing, we all sing,
Alleluia we all sing,
On Easter day!

First week of Lent

Getting ready

Theme

Jesus in the desert

Bible focus

When Jesus returned from the River Jordan, the power of the Holy Spirit was with him, and the Spirit led him into the desert. For forty days Jesus was tested by the devil.

LUKE 4:1–2

Story for the week

After Jesus had been baptized in the River Jordan, God's Spirit, the Holy Spirit, led him into the desert. Jesus was in the desert for 40 days. During that time he did not eat, and he was very hungry. The devil tried to make Jesus turn away from God by saying, 'If you are God's Son, tell this stone to turn into bread.' Jesus answered 'The Scriptures say, "No one can live only on food. You must also do as God says."' Then the devil led Jesus up to a high place and showed him all the nations of the world. The devil said that he would make Jesus king over all the earth if he worshipped the devil. Jesus answered, 'The Scriptures say, "Worship the Lord your God and serve only him!"' Then the devil took Jesus to stand on top of the temple in Jerusalem. The devil said, 'If you are God's Son, jump off. The Scriptures say that God will tell his angels to catch you so that you will not be hurt.' Jesus answered, 'The Scriptures also say, "Do not try to test the Lord your God!"' After the devil had finished testing Jesus, he went away. Jesus went back to Galilee, filled with the power of God's Holy Spirit.

Let's play and pray...

Story cloth activities

Monday

Jesus comes back from the River Jordan, full of the Holy Spirit.

Make a river out of foil or shiny material and place it on the cloth. Cut out and colour Jesus from the template on page 77 and stand him by the river.

Tuesday

Jesus is led by God's Holy Spirit into the desert.

Collect stones to make a stony desert and place them on the cloth. Place Jesus with the stones.

Wednesday

Jesus is hungry.

Place an empty plate next to Jesus.

Thursday

Jesus is offered the world.

Cut out and colour the world shape from the template on page 78 and stand it next to Jesus.

Friday

Jesus says, 'It is written in the Scriptures...'

Cut out and colour the Bible shape from the template on page 90 and stand it next to Jesus.

Saturday

Jesus returns to Galilee, filled with the power of God's Holy Spirit.

Move Jesus away from the stones. Cut out the dove shape from the template on page 85 and stand it next to Jesus.

Talk about

Monday Why is water so important for our lives?
Tuesday What might it be like to be in the desert?
Wednesday How does it feel to be hungry?
Thursday What does it feel like to be tempted?
Friday Talk about the Bible and why it is so important to us.
Saturday Talk about the dove as a symbol of the Holy Spirit.

Prayer for the week

Loving God, you sent your Holy Spirit to help Jesus when he was tempted in the desert. Send your Holy Spirit to help us every day. Amen

Song for the week

Jesus sat, all alone (Tune: This old man)
See page 68.

Year C

First week of Lent

Tune: This old man

Jesus sat, all alone,
In the desert on his own,
So the devil came and tempted him:
'Eat some bread if you are thin.'

Jesus said, 'Go away,
I'm not listening today.
You shall not live by bread alone,
Only God can make you whole.'

Jesus sat, all alone,
In the desert on his own,
So the devil tried a second time:
'Jump down from the temple high.'

Jesus said, 'Go away,
I'm not listening today.
For you shall not put God to the test.
Go away, you are a pest.'

Jesus sat, all alone,
In the desert on his own,
So the devil said, 'Come, worship me,
I will give you all you see.'

Jesus said, 'Go away,
I'm not listening today.
You're bound to know you cannot win.
Worship God and only him.'

Jesus sat, all alone,
In the desert on his own,
Where he was tempted, 1, 2, 3.
Now the devil's tempting me.

We will say, 'Go away,
We're not listening today.'
So let him put us to the test.
We all know that God is best!

Celebrating on Sunday

The first Sunday of Lent

Take to church

Take one of the stones you have collected to church.

Sunday worship

For the minister or worship leader

You will need:
- the desert cloth
- material to represent the river
- a bucket of extra stones for the congregation

During the service

The minister or worship leader may explore and develop the talking points, then say the prayer for the week, inviting people to bring stones to place on the cloth. The children may end this time by singing the song for the week (see page 68).

Second week of Lent

Getting ready

Theme
Jesus is warned about his death

Bible focus
Some Pharisees came and said to Jesus, 'You had better get away from here! Herod wants to kill you.'
LUKE 13:31

Story for the week
Jesus was busy. He was travelling around the villages and towns, teaching and healing people. Some religious people called Pharisees watched all that Jesus did. The Pharisees were jealous of Jesus and didn't like him because he did not keep all their rules. They didn't like what Jesus said. They didn't like the things he did. One day some Pharisees warned Jesus, 'Get away from here! King Herod wants to kill you.' Jesus said to them, 'Tell that fox Herod that I will stay here and keep on healing people until I am ready to go!' Then Jesus talked about the people who didn't believe in God or listen to his messengers. Jesus said, 'I want to look after them, like a hen gathering her chicks under her wings, but they won't let me.' Then Jesus said, 'I will go to Jerusalem when the time is right!'

Let's play and pray...

Story cloth activities

Monday
Some Pharisees warn Jesus that Herod wants to kill him.
Cut out and colour the sword shape from the template on page 91 and stand it beside Jesus.

Tuesday
Jesus says that he has not finished his work of healing.
Place a plaster on the cloth next to Jesus.

Wednesday
Jesus says that he will go to Jerusalem when he is ready.
Place a strip of material on the cloth to represent the road to Jerusalem. Stand Jesus on the road.

Thursday
Some people do not listen to God's messengers.
Cut out and colour the scroll shape from the template on page 91 and stand it next to Jesus.

Friday
Jesus wants to gather the people, as a hen gathers her chicks.
Cut out and colour two chick shapes from the template on page 91 and stand them beside Jesus.

Saturday
Jesus will go to Jerusalem when the time is right.
Move Jesus further along the road. Cut out and colour the Jerusalem shape from the template on page 78 and stand it at the far end of the cloth.

Talk about

- **Monday** Talk about what it feels like to be bullied and threatened.
- **Tuesday** Talk about how doctors and nurses help to heal people.
- **Wednesday** How do you get ready to go on a journey?
- **Thursday** Talk about people who bring messages.
- **Friday** Talk about how God cares for us and protects us.
- **Saturday** What does it feel like when you are waiting for things to happen?

Prayer for the week

Loving God, you sent your Son Jesus to show us how much you love us. Help us to be aware of your love surrounding us every day. Amen

Song for the week

Jesus came to heal and to save (Tune: Humpty Dumpty sat on a wall)
See page 69.

Year C

Second week of Lent

Tune: Humpty Dumpty sat on a wall

Jesus came to heal and to save,
And he is incredibly brave.
Though King Herod wants to kill him
Jesus will go to Jerusalem.
Jesus will go to Jerusalem.

Run from here now, Jesus is warned,
Herod is planning to murder you soon.
Though King Herod wants to kill him
Jesus will go to Jerusalem.
Jesus will go to Jerusalem.

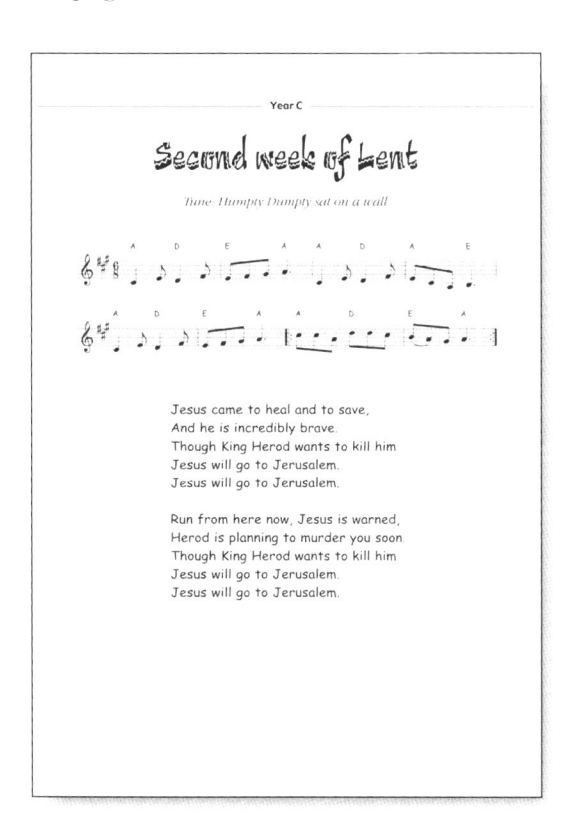

Celebrating on Sunday

The second Sunday of Lent

Take to church

Take a chick shape to church.

Sunday worship

For the minister or worship leader

> **You will need:**
> - extra chick shapes for the congregation

During the service

The minister or worship leader may explore and develop the talking points, then say the prayer for the week, inviting people to bring chick shapes to place on the cloth. The children may end this time by singing the song for the week (see page 69).

Year C

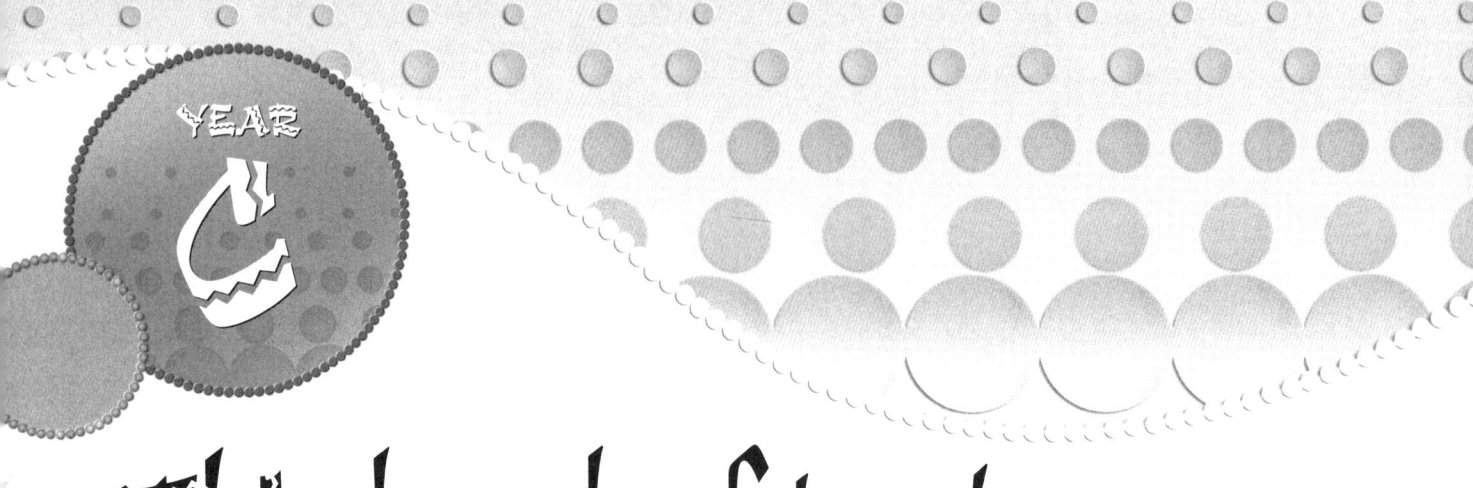

Third week of Lent

Getting ready

Theme

Jesus gives us a second chance

Bible focus

'Perhaps the tree will have figs on it next year. If it doesn't, you can have it cut down.'
LUKE 13:9

Story for the week

There were many people who did not obey God. Jesus said that God loved them and was patient, but he wanted these people to change their ways. God had given them lots of chances but one day it would be too late. There would be no more chances. Jesus told this story to explain what he meant:

One day a man planted a fig tree in good soil and waited patiently for the figs to grow. When he went to pick them, there were none. For three years he waited for the tree to grow figs, and still there were none. He grew impatient, and said to the gardener, 'Chop that tree down.' But the gardener pleaded, 'Wait just one more year.' The gardener promised to dig around the tree and put down some manure to make the figs grow. He said he would cut down the tree the next year if there were still no figs. So the tree had one last chance.

Let's play and pray...

Story cloth activities

Monday
Jesus says that people must change their ways.
   Cut out and colour the 'To God via Jesus' signpost from the template on page 92 and stand it next to Jesus on the road.

Tuesday
Jesus tells a story about a fig tree.
   Cut out and colour the fig tree shape from the template on page 92 and stand it next to Jesus.

Wednesday
The fig tree has no fruit.
   Cut out and colour the empty basket shape from the template on page 92 and stand it next to the tree.

Thursday
The man wants to cut down the fig tree.
   Cut out and colour the axe shape from the template on page 93 and stand it next to the tree.

Friday
The gardener says that he will feed the tree.
   Cut out and colour the watering can shape from the template on page 93 and stand it next to the tree.

Saturday
The gardener says, 'Give the tree just one more chance.'
   Cut out and colour two 'basket of fruit' shapes from the template on page 93 and stand them next to the tree. Move the axe and empty basket away.

Talk about

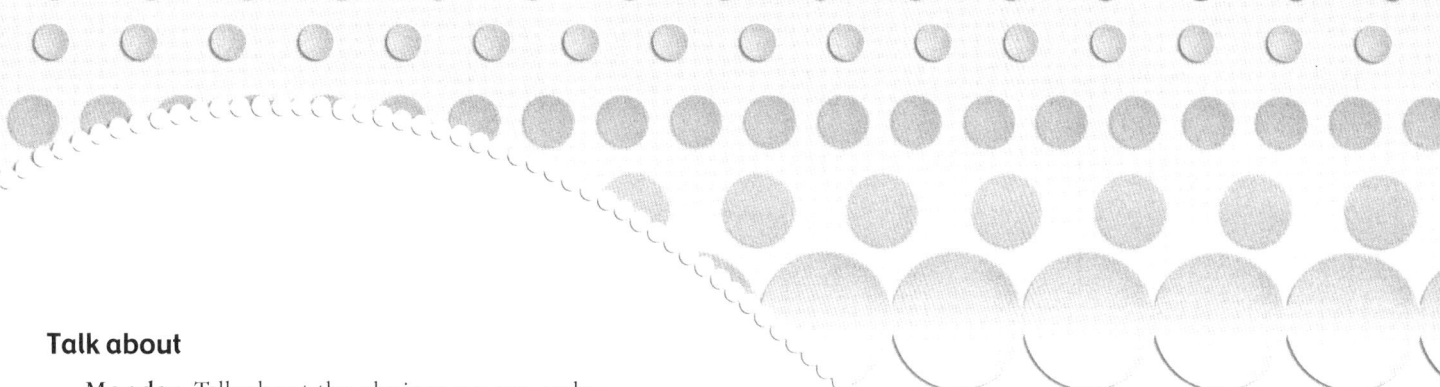

- **Monday** Talk about the choices we can make about the way we live.
- **Tuesday** Talk about fruit trees and fruit picking.
- **Wednesday** Why do crops fail?
- **Thursday** Why do we need to cut down trees?
- **Friday** Why must we feed and water plants?
- **Saturday** Why do we give people second chances?

Prayer for the week

Loving God, thank you that you give us a second chance when we do things wrong. Help us to give others a second chance when they behave badly towards us. Amen

Song for the week

I will plant a tree (Tune: Hokey Cokey)
See page 70.

Year C
Third week of Lent
Tune: Hokey Cokey

I will plant a tree
Because I want some fruit.
Good fruit, bad fruit,
Which one will it be?
I know I must be patient
And wait and wait and wait
And see if the good fruit grows.

Oh, will I have some good fruit?
Oh, will I have just no fruit?
Oh, will I have some good fruit?
Good fruit, no fruit,
Wait and see.

Celebrating on Sunday

The third Sunday of Lent

Take to church

Take a 'basket of fruit' shape to church.

Sunday worship

For the minister or worship leader

You will need:
- extra 'basket of fruit' shapes for the congregation

During the service

The minister or worship leader may explore and develop the talking points, then say the prayer for the week, inviting people to bring a basket of fruit to place on the cloth. The children may end this time by singing the song for the week (see page 70).

Fourth week of Lent

Getting ready

Theme
Jesus talks about love and forgiveness

Bible focus
'We should be glad and celebrate! Your brother was dead, but now he is alive. He was lost and has now been found.'
LUKE 15:32

Story for the week
The Pharisees didn't like Jesus. They didn't want Jesus to speak to people who had done wrong things. So Jesus told them this story to help them understand:

There was once a man who owned his own land. He had two sons. One day the younger son asked his father for his share of the money so that he could go away from home. The father divided all that he had between his two sons, and the younger one went away. For a while he had a lovely time, but then the money ran out and he had no friends. Worse still, there was a famine in the land and no food to spare. He went to work for a man who sent him out to look after the pigs. He was so hungry, he could even have eaten the pigs' food. At last, he came to his senses and decided to go home. His father saw him coming in the distance and ran to meet him with a big hug. He sent the servants to fetch good clothes, sandals for his son's feet and a ring for his finger. A big feast was also prepared. But the elder son was very angry and jealous. The father said, 'Be happy! Your brother, who we thought was dead, is alive. He was lost and now he is found.'

Let's play and pray...

Story cloth activities

Monday
Jesus tells a story about two sons.
Move Jesus along the road. Cut out and colour the crowd shape from the template on page 81 and stand it next to Jesus.

Tuesday
One son leaves, and spends all his money.
Cut out a circle of cloth, place some coins in it and tie it up with a piece of wool. Place it next to Jesus.

Wednesday
The son is so poor and hungry that he looks after pigs.
Cut out and colour the pig shape from the template on page 94 and stand it next to Jesus.

Thursday
The son decides to go home to his father.
Cut out and colour the father shape from the template on page 94 and stand it next to Jesus.

Friday
The father forgives his son and gives him the best of everything.
Cut out and colour ring shapes from the template on page 94. Stand them by the father.

Saturday
The elder son is angry.
Draw an angry face and place it next to the father.

Talk about

- **Monday** Why should brothers and sisters be good friends?
- **Tuesday** Why do we need to be careful with all that we have?
- **Wednesday** What might it feel like to have nothing?
- **Thursday** What does it feel like to come home?
- **Friday** Talk about why we must be forgiving.
- **Saturday** What does it feel like to be angry?

Prayer for the week

Loving God, you sent your Son Jesus to teach us how to forgive one another. Help us to forgive those who have hurt us. Amen

Song for the week

Farmer John, he had two sons (Tune: Jack and Jill)
See page 71.

Year C

Fourth week of Lent

Tune: Jack and Jill

Farmer John, he had two sons
Who did all that he taught them,
Until one day one went away
To spend his father's fortune.

The other son, he stayed at home
And worked hard for his money.
He had to work now twice as hard,
And didn't think this funny.

The lazy son, he went abroad
And soon spent all his money.
Then all his friends abandoned him
And he was rather lonely.

He packed his bags and left the pigs
And went back home to Daddy.
His father ran and welcomed him
And he was very happy.

'I'm sorry, Dad, I'll be your slave
If you will just forgive me.'
Said farmer John, 'Forget it, son,
You're home now and I'm happy.'

'My son was lost, now he is found,
Was dead, but now he's living.
I am your dad, and I am glad.
Of course you are forgiven.'

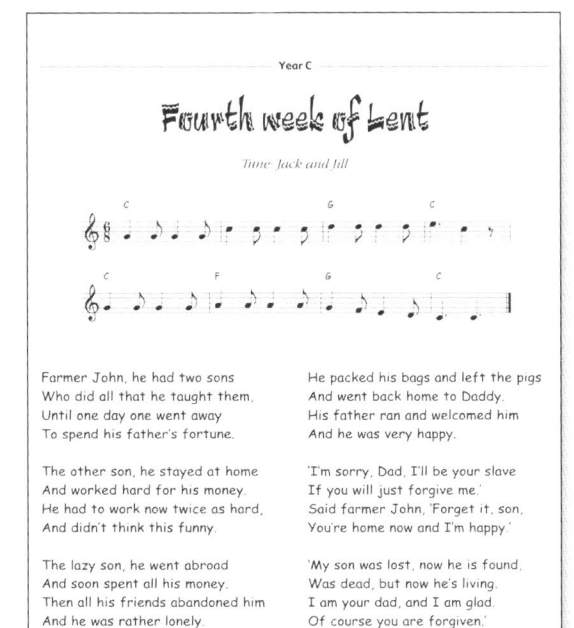

Celebrating on Sunday

The fourth Sunday of Lent (Mothering Sunday)

Take to church

Take a ring shape to church.

Sunday worship

For the minister or worship leader

> **You will need:**
> - extra ring shapes for the congregation

During the service

The minister or worship leader may explore and develop the talking points, then say the prayer for the week, inviting people to bring ring shapes to place on the cloth. The children may end this time by singing the song for the week (see page 71).

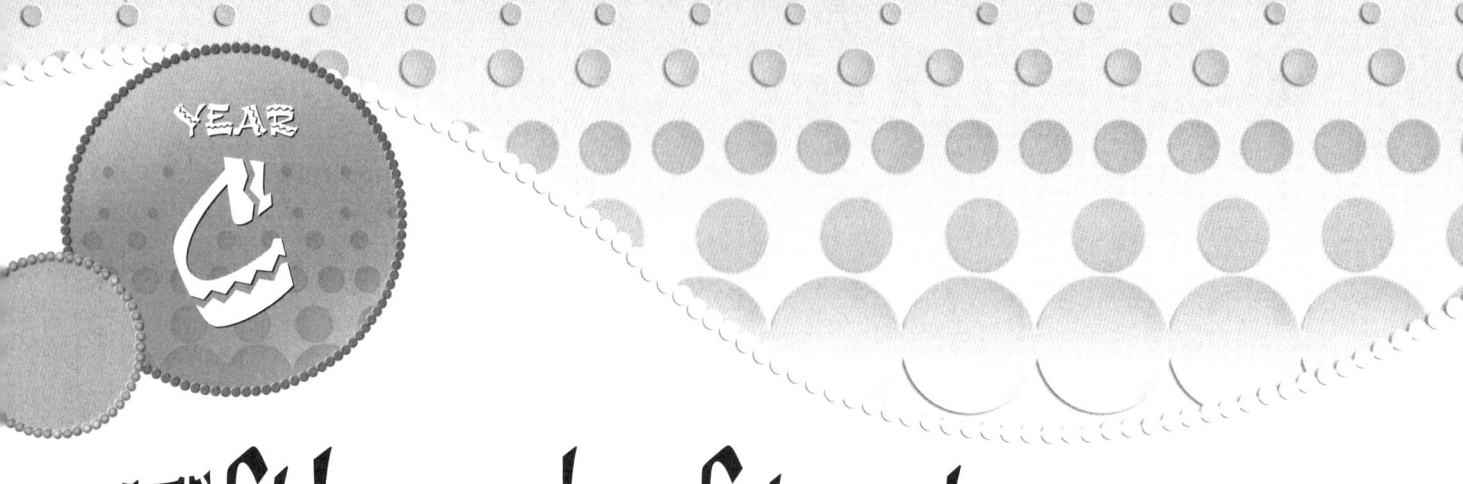

Fifth week of Lent

Getting ready

Theme
Jesus talks about his death

Bible focus
Jesus said, 'Leave her alone! She has kept this perfume for the day of my burial.'
JOHN 12:7

Story for the week
Jesus was visiting his friends at Bethany. There was Martha, her sister Mary and their brother Lazarus. Jesus, Lazarus and the disciples were all eating together. Martha was busy cooking in the kitchen and serving the food. Suddenly, Mary came into the room carrying a bottle of expensive perfume. She knelt down and poured the perfume over Jesus' feet. Then, she wiped his feet with her long hair. You could smell the perfume all over the house.

Now one of the disciples, called Judas, looked after the disciples' money. He was not very happy. 'What a waste of money,' he moaned. 'We could have sold that perfume and given the money to the poor.' But Jesus replied, 'Leave Mary alone. She did this because she loves me. She has kept this perfume for my burial. You will always have poor people with you, but I won't be here much longer.'

Let's play and pray...

Story cloth activities

Monday
Jesus visits his friends at Bethany.
Cut out and colour the Bethany house shape from the template on page 95 and stand it further along the road. Stand Jesus next to it.

Tuesday
Jesus and his disciples stay for a meal.
Place a spoon next to Jesus.

Wednesday
Martha serves the food.
Place some small tins of food next to Jesus.

Thursday
Mary anoints Jesus' feet with perfume.
Cut out and colour the feet shape from the template on page 95 and place some pot-pourri next to it.

Friday
Judas Iscariot is angry at the waste.
Cut out and colour some denarius coins from the template on page 95 and stand them next to Jesus.

Saturday
Jesus talks about his burial.
Place the green (garden) cloth alongside the desert cloth. Cut out and colour the tomb and stone shapes from the template on page 82 and stand them with the pot-pourri at the join between the two cloths.

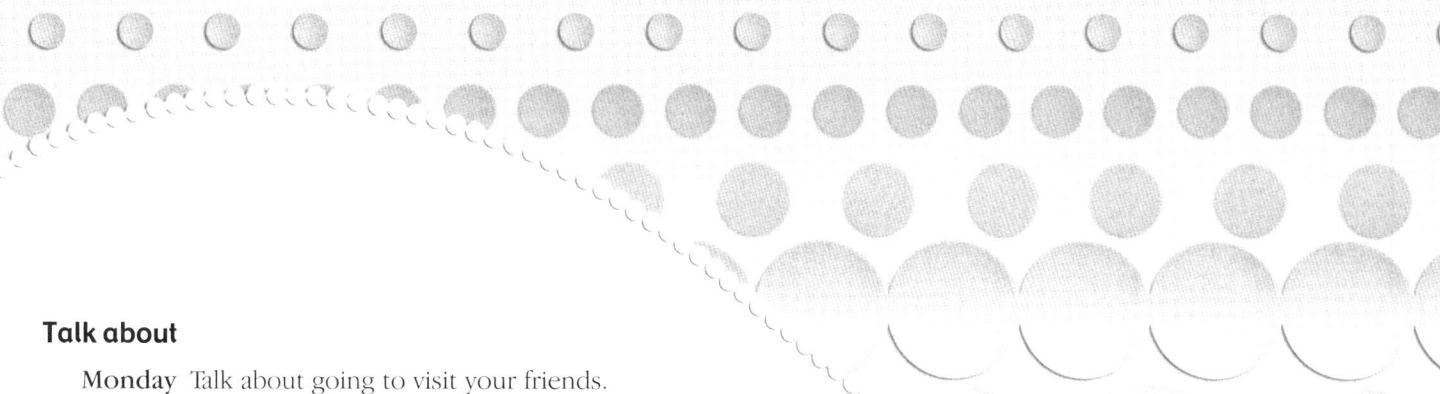

Talk about

- Monday Talk about going to visit your friends.
- Tuesday Talk about going out for a meal.
- Wednesday What are your favourite foods?
- Thursday What smells do you like best?
- Friday Why shouldn't we waste things?
- Saturday Why do people go to funerals?

Prayer for the week

Loving God, your Son Jesus taught us to be thankful when people are kind to us. Help us always to remember to say 'thank you'. Amen

Song for the week

Jesus went to see his friends (Tune: Have you seen the muffin man?)
See page 72.

Year C

Fifth week of Lent

Tune: Have you seen the muffin man?

Jesus went to see his friends,
To see his friends,
To see his friends.
Jesus went to see his friends
And they ate a meal together.

Mary took her best perfume,
Her best perfume,
Her best perfume.
Mary took her best perfume
And knelt down on the floor.

She poured it all on Jesus' feet,
On Jesus' feet,
On Jesus' feet.
She poured it all on Jesus' feet
And wiped them with her hair.

Judas tried to tell her off,
To tell her off,
To tell her off.
Judas tried to tell her off,
'That really was a waste.'

Jesus thanked her for her care,
For all her care,
For all her care.
Jesus thanked her for her care
In looking after him.

Celebrating on Sunday

The fifth Sunday of Lent

Take to church

Take some pot-pourri to church.

Sunday worship

For the minister or worship leader

> **You will need:**
> ✪ extra pot-pourri for the congregation

During the service

The minister or worship leader may explore and develop the talking points, then say the prayer for the week, inviting people to bring pot-pourri to place on the cloth. The children may end this time by singing the song for the week (see page 72).

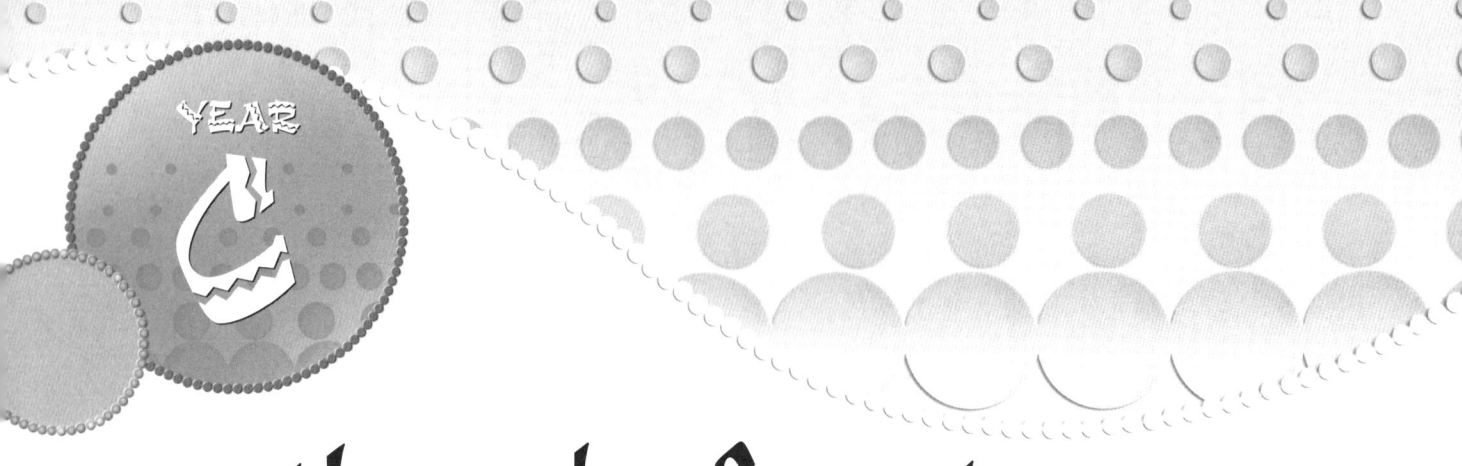

Sixth week of Lent

Getting ready

Theme
Jesus dies on the cross

Bible focus
Jesus shouted, 'Father, I put myself in your hands!' Then he died.

LUKE 23:46

Story for the week

From Bethany, Jesus went into Jerusalem. There, Jesus had his last meal with his disciples. Then Jesus went into the garden to pray. Soldiers arrested Jesus when he was praying in the garden. The religious leaders questioned him and sent him to Pilate. Then Pilate sent Jesus to Herod. Herod and his soldiers made fun of Jesus and insulted him. They put a fine robe on him and sent him back to Pilate. Herod and Pilate became friends, even though they had always been enemies before this.

Pilate wanted to set Jesus free, but the crowd kept shouting, 'Nail him to a cross! Nail him to a cross!' Pilate gave in and Jesus was led away by the soldiers. When they came to the place called 'The Skull', they nailed Jesus to a cross. They also nailed two criminals to crosses, one on each side of Jesus. The soldiers made fun of Jesus and brought him some wine. At midday the sky turned dark and the sun stopped shining. Jesus died. All of Jesus' close friends and the women who had come with him from Galilee stood at a distance and watched.

Let's play and pray...

Story cloth activities

Monday
Herod and his soldiers make fun of Jesus.
Move Jerusalem to the far side of the green cloth and stand Jesus next to it. Drape a piece of material around Jesus to make an elegant robe.

Tuesday
Herod and Pilate become friends.
Make two friendship bracelets by plaiting wool, and place them on the cloth.

Wednesday
They crucify Jesus along with two criminals.
Cut out three cross shapes from the template on page 78 and stand them next to Jesus.

Thursday
The soldiers offer Jesus wine vinegar to drink.
Sprinkle some wine vinegar (or any vinegar) on to some cottonwool and place it next to Jesus.

Friday
Darkness comes over the whole land.
Cover the whole cloth with a piece of dark purple material.

Saturday
All those who know Jesus stand at a distance and watch.
Remove the dark cloth and place the crowd a little distance from the crosses.

Talk about

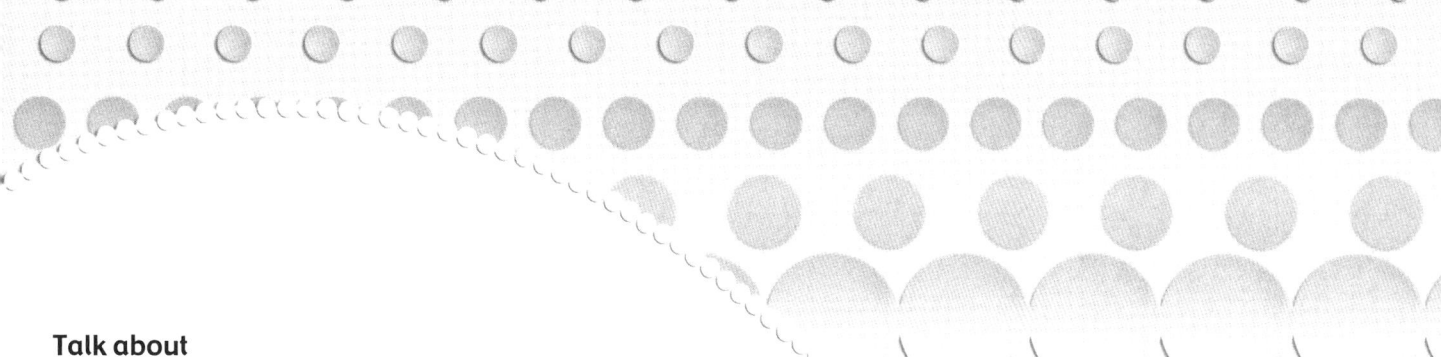

- Monday — How does it feel when people make fun of you?
- Tuesday — Talk about what makes a good friend.
- Wednesday — Talk about the cross as a symbol of the Christian faith.
- Thursday — How does it feel to be thirsty?
- Friday — Talk about how it feels to be in the dark.
- Saturday — Talk about how Jesus' friends and disciples might be feeling as they watch him die.

Prayer for the week

Loving God, your Son Jesus suffered and died on the cross. Help us to know that Jesus shares our suffering. Amen

Song for the week

There was a man named Pontius Pilate (Tune: Michael Finnegan)
See page 73.

Year C

Sixth week of Lent

Tune: Michael Finnegan

There was a man named Pontius Pilate,
He was cruel and sometimes violent.
They brought him Jesus on Good Friday.
Pilate got it wrong again, wrong again.
Pilate got it wrong again, wrong again.

Pilate sent Jesus off to Herod,
'You're the king, now he's your problem.'
Herod laughed and he mocked Jesus.
Herod got it wrong again, wrong again.
Herod got it wrong again, wrong again.

King Herod sent him back to Pilate,
'He's no king; he's no messiah!
Why not let them crucify him?'
Herod got it wrong again, wrong again.
Herod got it wrong again, wrong again.

Pilate washed his hands of Jesus
While they shouted, 'Crucify him!'
Soldiers stripped and whipped him cruelly.
Pilate got it wrong again, wrong again.
Pilate got it wrong again, wrong again.

As Jesus died he said, 'Forgive them,
They don't know what they are doing.'
Bowed his head, gave up his spirit.
His friends, they stood and cried again, cried again.
His friends, they stood and cried again, cried again.

It went dark, the world was silent.
All this happened on Good Friday.
Jesus died and he was buried.
There he lay till Easter Day again, then rose again.
There he lay till Easter Day again, then rose again.

Celebrating on Sunday

The sixth Sunday of Lent (Palm Sunday)

Take to church

Take a friendship bracelet to church.

Sunday worship

For the minister or worship leader

You will need:
- some lengths of wool or ready-made friendship bracelets for the congregation

During the service

The minister or worship leader may explore and develop the talking points, then say the prayer for the week, inviting people to bring friendship bracelets or wool to place on the cloth. The children may end this time by singing the song for the week (see page 73).

YEAR C

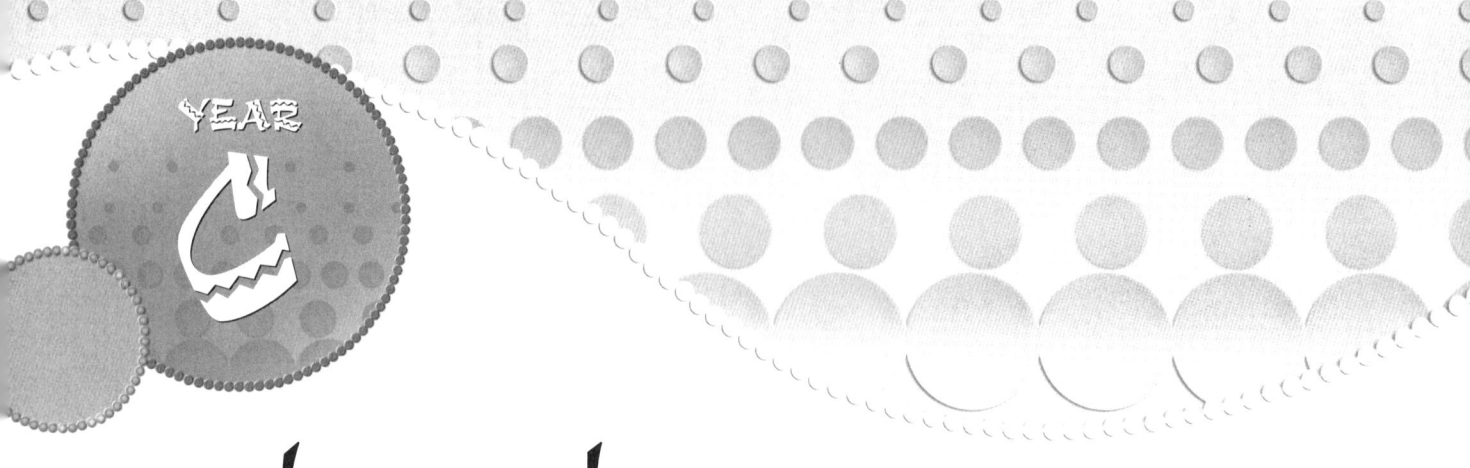

Holy Week

Getting ready

Theme
Jesus is alive

Bible focus
Mary Magdalene then went and told the disciples that she had seen the Lord.
JOHN 20:18

Story for the week
When Jesus died on the cross, his friends put his body into a tomb with a stone over the doorway. Early on Sunday morning, when it was still dark, Mary Magdalene went to the tomb. She took perfume and spices to anoint Jesus' body. When Mary got there, the stone had been moved away and Jesus was gone. Mary ran and told Peter and John, 'Jesus' body has gone!' Then Peter and John raced to the tomb as fast as their legs would carry them. John got there first. He looked in and saw just folded clothes. But Peter went inside. Peter and John went straight back home. Mary stayed, weeping beside the tomb. Then she saw a man. He asked her, 'Why are you crying?' Then he called out her name: 'Mary!' It was Jesus! Mary was so happy. She ran and told the disciples, 'I have seen Jesus. He is alive!'

Let's play and pray...

Story cloth activities

Monday
Jesus dies and is placed in the tomb.
   Place Jesus in the box. Move the tomb to Jerusalem and cover the entrance with the stone.

Tuesday
Mary Magdalene visits the tomb and finds it empty.
   Move the stone away from the tomb. Cut out and colour the Mary Magdalene shape from the template on page 96 and stand it next to the tomb.

Wednesday
Mary goes to tell Peter and John.
   Cut out and colour the Peter and John shapes from the template on page 96 and stand them in Jerusalem. Move Mary to join them.

Thursday
John sees the empty tomb with the folded clothes.
   Place John next to the tomb.

Friday
Peter goes into the tomb.
   Move Peter to the tomb. Place a small piece of cloth or bandage at the tomb.

Saturday
Mary sees Jesus and knows that he is alive.
   Stand Jesus in the centre of the cloth with Mary. Cut out and colour some flower shapes from the template on page 89 to place around them.

Talk about

- Monday — Why do people bring flowers when someone dies?
- Tuesday — How might Mary have felt when she saw the empty tomb?
- Wednesday — How did Peter and John feel when Mary told them that Jesus had gone?
- Thursday — Talk about finding things out for yourself.
- Friday — Talk about believing in Jesus.
- Saturday — Talk about being happy and joyful because Jesus is alive.

Prayer for the week

Loving God, your Son Jesus died, was buried and has risen again. Help us to know that Jesus is alive and always with us. Amen

Song for the week

I have seen the Lord (Tune: The farmer's in his den)
See page 74.

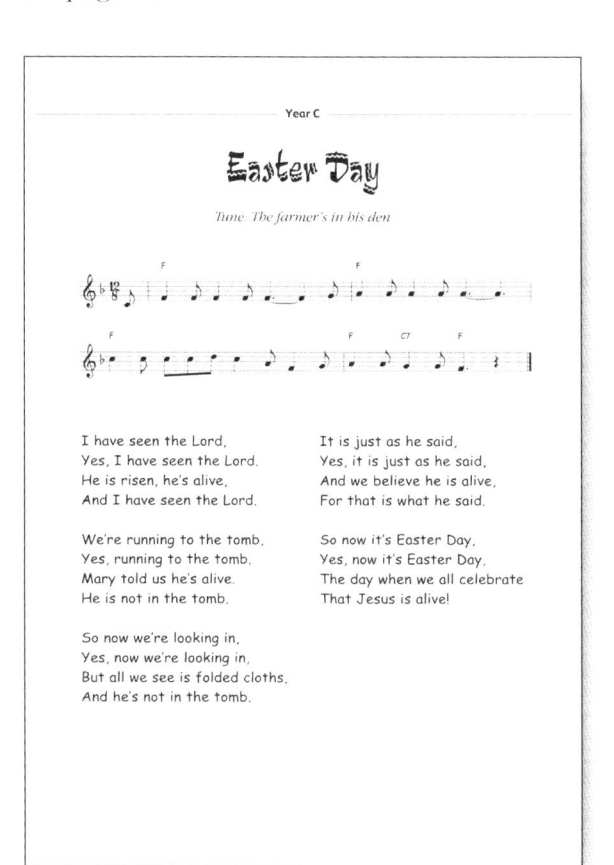

Year C

Easter Day

Tune: The farmer's in his den

I have seen the Lord,
Yes, I have seen the Lord.
He is risen, he's alive,
And I have seen the Lord.

We're running to the tomb,
Yes, running to the tomb.
Mary told us he's alive.
He is not in the tomb.

So now we're looking in,
Yes, now we're looking in,
But all we see is folded cloths,
And he's not in the tomb.

It is just as he said,
Yes, it is just as he said,
And we believe he is alive,
For that is what he said.

So now it's Easter Day,
Yes, now it's Easter Day,
The day when we all celebrate
That Jesus is alive!

Celebrating on Sunday

Easter Day

Take to church

Take a flower shape or some fresh flowers to church.

Sunday worship

For the minister or worship leader

> **You will need:**
> - a flower shape or some fresh flowers for each member of the congregation

During the service

The minister or worship leader may explore and develop the talking points, then say the prayer for the week, inviting people to place a flower shape or some fresh flowers on the green (garden) cloth. The children may end this time by singing the song for the week (see page 74).

SONGS for the week

Year A

First week of Lent

Tune: This old man

Jesus sat, all alone,
In the desert on his own,
So the devil came and tempted him:
'Eat some bread if you are thin.'

Jesus said, 'Go away,
I'm not listening today.
You shall not live by bread alone,
Only God can make you whole.'

Jesus sat, all alone,
In the desert on his own,
So the devil tried a second time:
'Jump down from the temple high.'

Jesus said, 'Go away,
I'm not listening today.
For you shall not put God to the test.
Go away, you are a pest.'

Jesus sat, all alone,
In the desert on his own,
So the devil said, 'Come, worship me,
I will give you all you see.'

Jesus said, 'Go away,
I'm not listening today.
You're bound to know you cannot win.
Worship God and only him.'

Jesus sat, all alone,
In the desert on his own,
Where he was tempted, 1, 2, 3.
Now the devil's tempting me.

We will say, 'Go away,
We're not listening today.'
So let him put us to the test.
We all know that God is best!

Year A

Second week of Lent

Tune: The Grand Old Duke of York

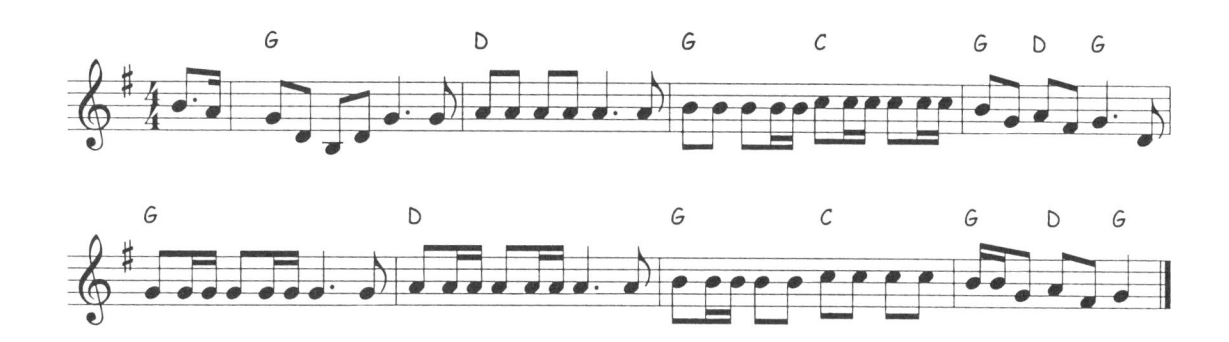

We know God so loved the world
That he gave his only Son,
And if you will only believe in him
You will have eternal life.

Nicodemus wasn't sure,
So he came to find out more.
Jesus told him straight,
if you will be saved,
Then you must be born again.

Because God so loved the world,
He gave his only Son,
And if you will only believe in him
You will have eternal life.

Born of water from above
And the Spirit of God's love,
That's a gift to all who on Jesus call,
Wanting to be born again.

Because God so loved the world,
He gave his only Son,
And if you will only believe in him
You will have eternal life.

Year A

Third week of Lent

Tune: If you're happy and you know it

When you're thirsty and you know it, have a drink.
When you're thirsty and you know it, have a drink.
When you're thirsty and you know it, and you really want to show it,
When you're thirsty and you know it, have a drink.

Jesus is the living water, come to him.
Jesus is the living water, come to him.
Jesus is the living water, and we all know what he taught us,
Jesus is the living water, come to him.

And if you will turn to Jesus, you will live.
And if you will turn to Jesus, you will live.
And if you will turn to Jesus as a modern-day believer,
Yes, if you will turn to Jesus, you will live.

Year A

Fourth week of Lent

Tune: She'll be coming round the mountain

Jesus met a blind man sitting by the road.
Jesus met a blind man sitting by the road.
Jesus met a blind man sitting, met a blind man sitting,
Met a blind man sitting by the road.

Jesus cured him with some spit and some mud.
Jesus cured him with some spit and some mud.
Jesus cured him with some spit, cured him with some spit,
Cured him with some spit and some mud.

And now he can see the Son of God.
And now he can see the Son of God.
With his eyes wide open, eyes wide open,
Now he can see the Son of God.

— Year A —

Fifth week of Lent

Tune: Old MacDonald

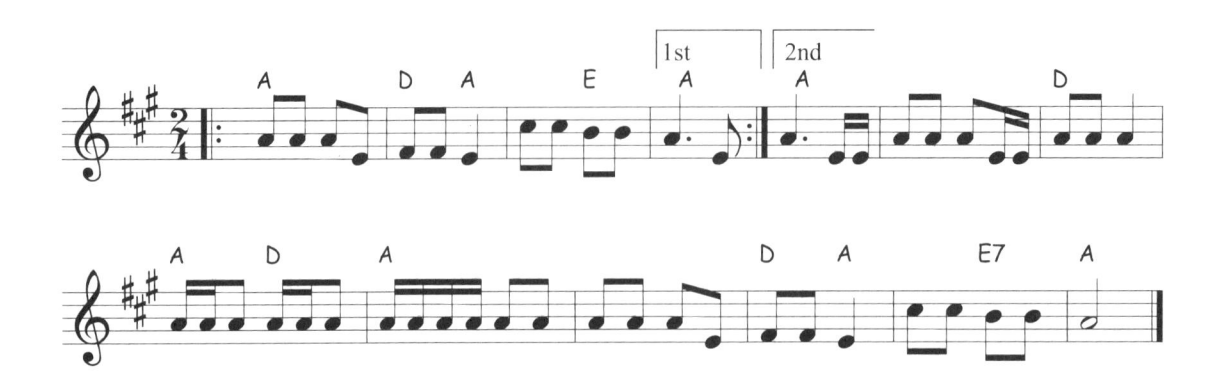

Lazarus was very ill,
Oh, my dear, oh no!
His sisters thought that he would die,
Oh, my dear, oh no!

He was going pale,
he was getting weak,
First a cough, then a chill,
then he had to go to bed.
Lazarus was very ill,
Oh, my dear, oh no!

Lazarus died in his bed,
Oh, my dear, oh no!
His sisters stood around and cried,
Oh, my dear, oh no!

Then they found a tomb,
And they buried him,
Sealed him up, in the ground
While his sisters stood around.
Lazarus was really dead,
Oh, my dear, oh no!

Lazarus was Jesus' friend,
Yes, my dear, oh yes!
Jesus came and gave him life,
Yes, my dear, oh yes!

And he wasn't pale,
And he wasn't weak,
He was strong, and full of life,
And so glad to be alive.
Lazarus came back to life,
Yes, my dear, oh yes!

Sixth week of Lent

Tune: Baa Baa Black Sheep

Take, eat this bread, it is my body,
When you eat it, think of me.
Give some to Peter, James and John,
To all the disciples in this room.

Take, drink my blood, I give for you,
Please remember what I do.
Give some to Peter, James and John,
To all the disciples in this room.

On Thursday, in the upper room,
Jesus left a gift for you.
Holy communion, bread and wine,
We share his meal together in this room.

Year A

Easter Day

Tune: Happy birthday to you

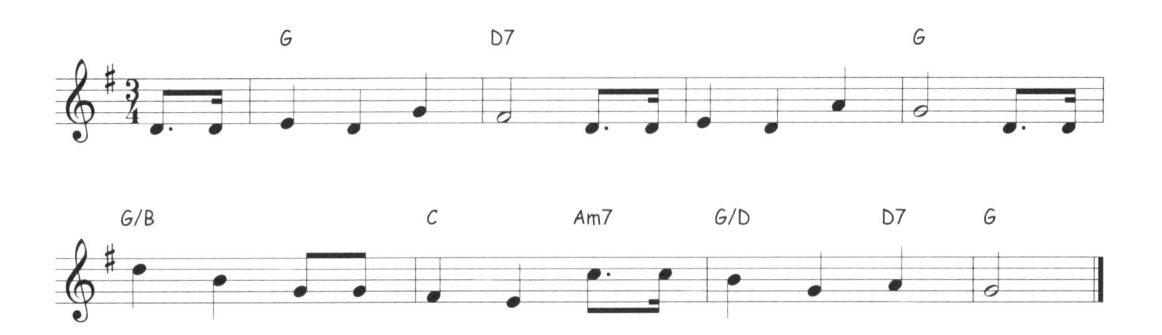

Let us go to the tomb,
Full of sadness and gloom.
Let us go and bury Jesus,
Let us go to the tomb.

But the stone did not stay,
It has been rolled away,
And we wonder what has happened
On this first Easter Day.

Then we're really amazed
And our hearts fill with praise.
He is risen! Alleluia!
Our Lord Jesus is raised.

Alleluia we sing
To Lord Jesus, our king.
Alleluia, he is risen,
Alleluia we sing.

It's a birthday today
In a very special way,
For our new life that's eternal
Started on Easter Day.

Year B

First week of Lent

Tune: The animals marched in two by two, hurrah, hurrah!

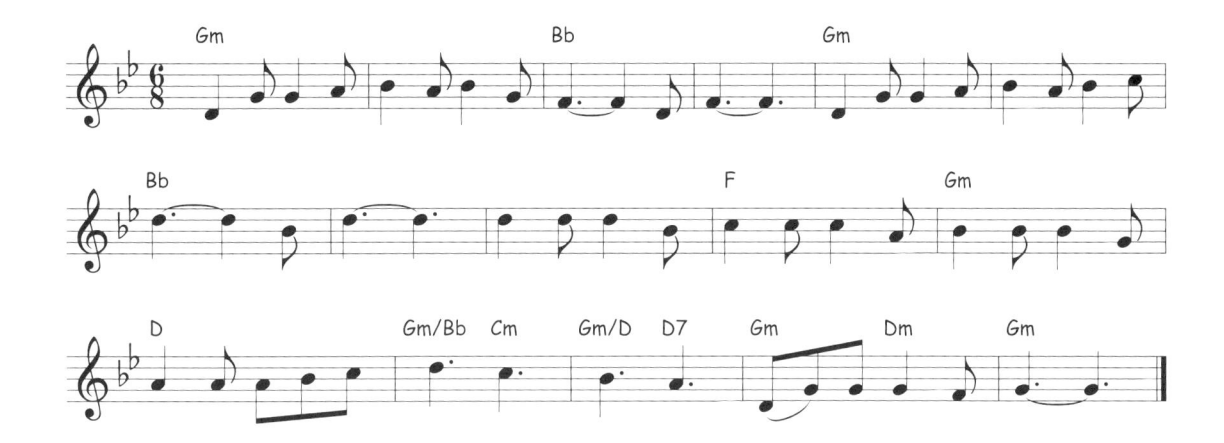

Jesus needed time alone—to pray, to pray.
Jesus needed time alone—to pray, to pray.
Jesus needed time to pray
So all alone he went away,
And God's angels came to take great care of him.

Jesus prayed for forty days—to God, to God.
Jesus prayed for forty days—to God, to God.
Jesus prayed for forty days
In the desert where he stayed,
And God's angels came to take great care of him.

Satan tempted God's own Son—O dear, O dear.
Satan tempted God's own Son—O dear, O dear.
Satan tempted God's own Son,
He tried and tried, but Jesus won,
And God's angels came to take great care of him.

The angels came to bring him food—hurrah, hurrah.
The angels came to bring him food—hurrah, hurrah.
The angels came to bring him food,
For Jesus is the Son of God,
Yes, God's angels came to take great care of him.

Second week of Lent

Tune: Ten green bottles

Choose one child as Jesus. Jesus starts walking while all the other children sing the song. At the appropriate time, Jesus chooses a child ('N') to walk with him. The child's name is inserted and the song carries on. The verse can be repeated as many times as necessary; one new child joins the chain for each repetition. Eventually all of the children will be walking with Jesus.

Jesus is going to Jerusalem,
Jesus is going to Jerusalem,
And if 'N' can carry a cross and follow him
Then he'll (she'll) be going all the way to heaven.

Third week of Lent

Tune: The wheels on the bus

My Father's house is a house of prayer,
House of prayer,
House of prayer.
My Father's house is a house of prayer
All day long.

You have made it a den of thieves,
Den of thieves,
Den of thieves.
You have made it a den of thieves
All day long.

Tip the tables, spill the coins,
Spill the coins,
Spill the coins.
Tip the tables, spill the coins
All day long.

Now it's quiet, we can pray,
We can pray,
We can pray.
Now it's quiet, we can pray
All day long.

Year B

Fourth week of Lent

Tune: The farmer's in his den

We have to make a choice,
We have to make a choice,
Follow Jesus, or walk away,
We have to make a choice.

We're walking down the road,
We're walking down the road,
Follow Jesus, or walk away,
We're walking down the road.

One way leads to life,
One way leads to life,
Follow Jesus, or walk away,
Just one way leads to life.

We're walking in the light,
We're walking in the light,
Jesus wants to save us all,
We're walking in the light.

Fifth week of Lent

Tune: Three blind mice

One small seed, one small seed,
See how it grows, see how it grows.
It grows so tall in the morning light,
It goes on growing throughout the night.
Did you ever see such a thing in your life
As one small seed?

One small seed, one small seed,
Laid in the ground, laid in the ground.
It grows so tall in the morning light,
It goes on growing throughout the night.
Did you ever see such a thing in your life
As one small seed?

One small seed, one small seed,
What will it be, what will it be?
It grows so tall in the morning light,
It goes on growing throughout the night.
Did you ever see such a thing in your life
As one small seed?

One small child, one small child,
See how we grow, see how we grow.
We grow so tall in the love of God,
We know he loves us, for he is good.
He'll go on loving throughout our life
With his true love.

Sixth week of Lent

Tune: One man went to mow

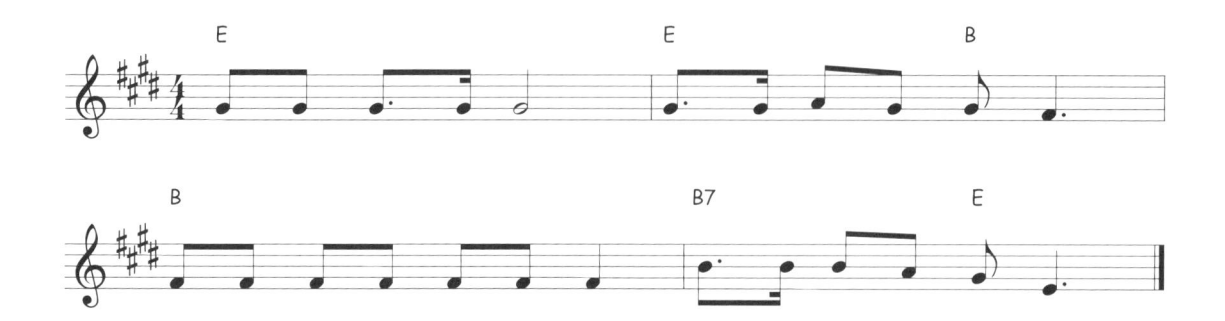

Jesus came to town
Riding on a donkey.
Jesus with his followers
Came into the city.

Jesus came to town
Riding on a donkey.
Jesus with his followers
Waving tall palm branches.

Jesus came to town
Riding on a donkey.
Jesus with his followers
Throwing down their jackets.

Jesus came to town
Riding on a donkey.
Jesus with his followers
Shouting loud hosannas.

Jesus came to town
Riding on a donkey.
Jesus with his followers
Shouting, 'Jesus, save us.'

Jesus came to town
Riding on a donkey.
Jesus with his followers
Shouting loud hosannas.

Year B

Easter Day

Tune: Here we go round the mulberry bush

Thank you, God, for Easter day,
Easter day, Easter day,
Thank you, God, for Easter day,
Now we are saved.

Alleluia we all sing,
We all sing, we all sing,
Alleluia we all sing,
On Easter day.

Jesus isn't in the tomb,
In the tomb, in the tomb,
Jesus isn't in the tomb,
Let's sing his praise.

Alleluia, shout for joy,
Shout for joy, shout for joy,
Alleluia, shout for joy,
And sing his praise.

Jesus is alive today,
Alive today, alive today,
Jesus is alive today,
Let's sing his praise.

Alleluia, tell the world,
Tell the world, tell the world,
Alleluia, tell the world,
To sing his praise.

Jesus is the Son of God,
Son of God, Son of God,
Jesus is the Son of God,
Let's sing his praise.

Alleluia we all sing,
We all sing, we all sing,
Alleluia we all sing,
On Easter day!

Year C

First week of Lent

Tune: This old man

Jesus sat, all alone,
In the desert on his own,
So the devil came and tempted him:
'Eat some bread if you are thin.'

Jesus said, 'Go away,
I'm not listening today.
You shall not live by bread alone,
Only God can make you whole.'

Jesus sat, all alone,
In the desert on his own,
So the devil tried a second time:
'Jump down from the temple high.'

Jesus said, 'Go away,
I'm not listening today.
For you shall not put God to the test.
Go away, you are a pest.'

Jesus sat, all alone,
In the desert on his own,
So the devil said, 'Come, worship me,
I will give you all you see.'

Jesus said, 'Go away,
I'm not listening today.
You're bound to know you cannot win.
Worship God and only him.'

Jesus sat, all alone,
In the desert on his own,
Where he was tempted, 1, 2, 3.
Now the devil's tempting me.

We will say, 'Go away,
We're not listening today.'
So let him put us to the test.
We all know that God is best!

Second week of Lent

Tune: Humpty Dumpty sat on a wall

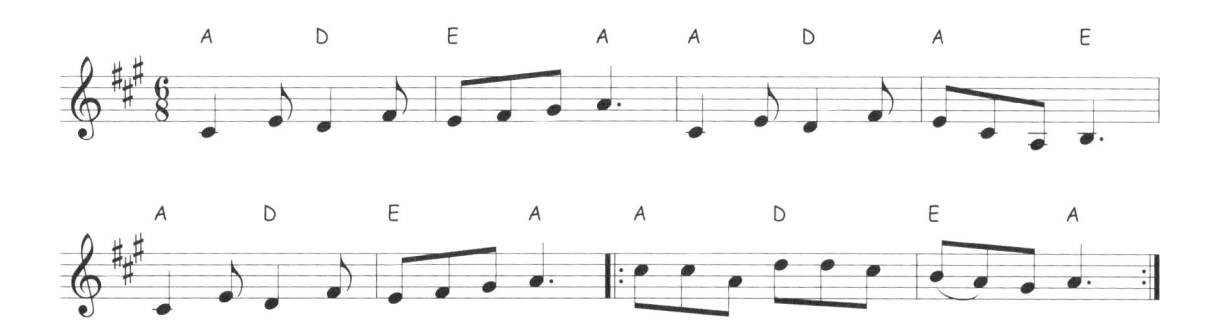

Jesus came to heal and to save,
And he is incredibly brave.
Though King Herod wants to kill him
Jesus will go to Jerusalem.
Jesus will go to Jerusalem.

Run from here now, Jesus is warned,
Herod is planning to murder you soon.
Though King Herod wants to kill him
Jesus will go to Jerusalem.
Jesus will go to Jerusalem.

Year C

Third week of Lent

Tune: Hokey Cokey

I will plant a tree
Because I want some fruit.
Good fruit, bad fruit,
Which one will it be?
I know I must be patient
And wait and wait and wait
And see if the good fruit grows.

Oh, will I have some good fruit?
Oh, will I have just no fruit?
Oh, will I have some good fruit?
Good fruit, no fruit,
Wait and see.

Fourth week of Lent

Tune: Jack and Jill

Farmer John, he had two sons
Who did all that he taught them,
Until one day one went away
To spend his father's fortune.

The other son, he stayed at home
And worked hard for his money.
He had to work now twice as hard,
And didn't think this funny.

The lazy son, he went abroad
And soon spent all his money.
Then all his friends abandoned him
And he was rather lonely.

He packed his bags and left the pigs
And went back home to Daddy.
His father ran and welcomed him
And he was very happy.

'I'm sorry, Dad, I'll be your slave
If you will just forgive me.'
Said farmer John, 'Forget it, son,
You're home now and I'm happy.'

'My son was lost, now he is found,
Was dead, but now he's living.
I am your dad, and I am glad.
Of course you are forgiven.'

Year C

Fifth week of Lent

Tune: Have you seen the muffin man?

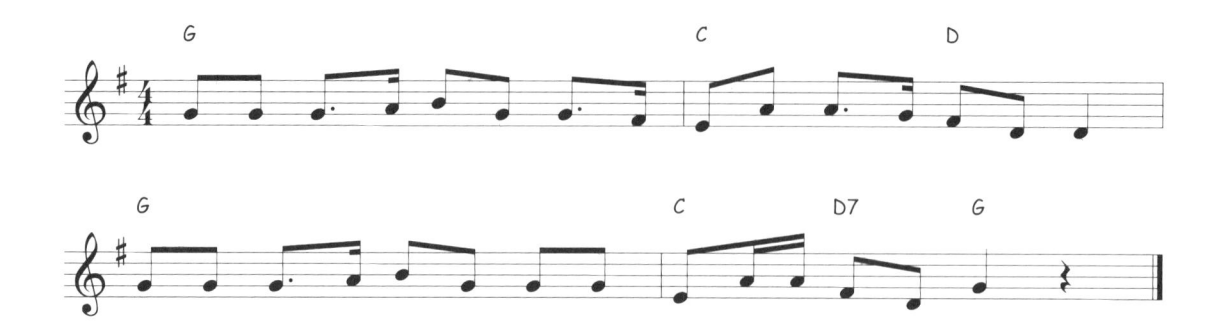

Jesus went to see his friends,
To see his friends,
To see his friends.
Jesus went to see his friends
And they ate a meal together.

Mary took her best perfume,
Her best perfume,
Her best perfume.
Mary took her best perfume
And knelt down on the floor.

She poured it all on Jesus' feet,
On Jesus' feet,
On Jesus' feet.
She poured it all on Jesus' feet
And wiped them with her hair.

Judas tried to tell her off,
To tell her off,
To tell her off.
Judas tried to tell her off,
'That really was a waste.'

Jesus thanked her for her care,
For all her care,
For all her care.
Jesus thanked her for her care
In looking after him.

Year C

Sixth week of Lent

Tune: Michael Finnegan

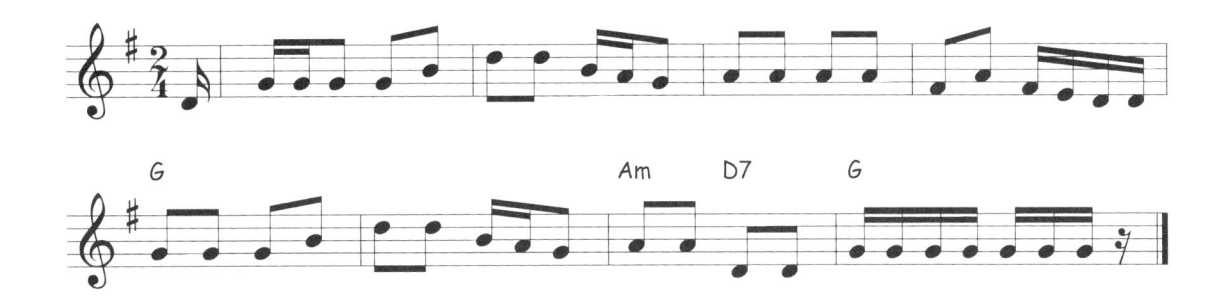

There was a man named Pontius Pilate,
He was cruel and sometimes violent.
They brought him Jesus on Good Friday.
Pilate got it wrong again, wrong again.
Pilate got it wrong again, wrong again.

Pilate sent Jesus off to Herod,
'You're the king, now he's your problem.'
Herod laughed and he mocked Jesus.
Herod got it wrong again, wrong again.
Herod got it wrong again, wrong again.

King Herod sent him back to Pilate,
'He's no king; he's no messiah!
Why not let them crucify him?'
Herod got it wrong again, wrong again.
Herod got it wrong again, wrong again.

Pilate washed his hands of Jesus
While they shouted, 'Crucify him!'
Soldiers stripped and whipped him cruelly.
Pilate got it wrong again, wrong again.
Pilate got it wrong again, wrong again.

As Jesus died he said, 'Forgive them.
They don't know what they are doing.'
Bowed his head, gave up his spirit.
His friends, they stood and cried again, cried again.
His friends, they stood and cried again, cried again.

It went dark, the world was silent.
All this happened on Good Friday.
Jesus died and he was buried.
There he lay till Easter Day again, then rose again.
There he lay till Easter Day again, then rose again.

Easter Day

Tune: The farmer's in his den

I have seen the Lord,
Yes, I have seen the Lord.
He is risen, he's alive,
And I have seen the Lord.

We're running to the tomb,
Yes, running to the tomb.
Mary told us he's alive.
He is not in the tomb.

So now we're looking in,
Yes, now we're looking in,
But all we see is folded cloths,
And he's not in the tomb.

It is just as he said,
Yes, it is just as he said,
And we believe he is alive,
For that is what he said.

So now it's Easter Day,
Yes, now it's Easter Day,
The day when we all celebrate
That Jesus is alive!

TEMPLATES

Year A

First week of Lent

Temple

Mountain

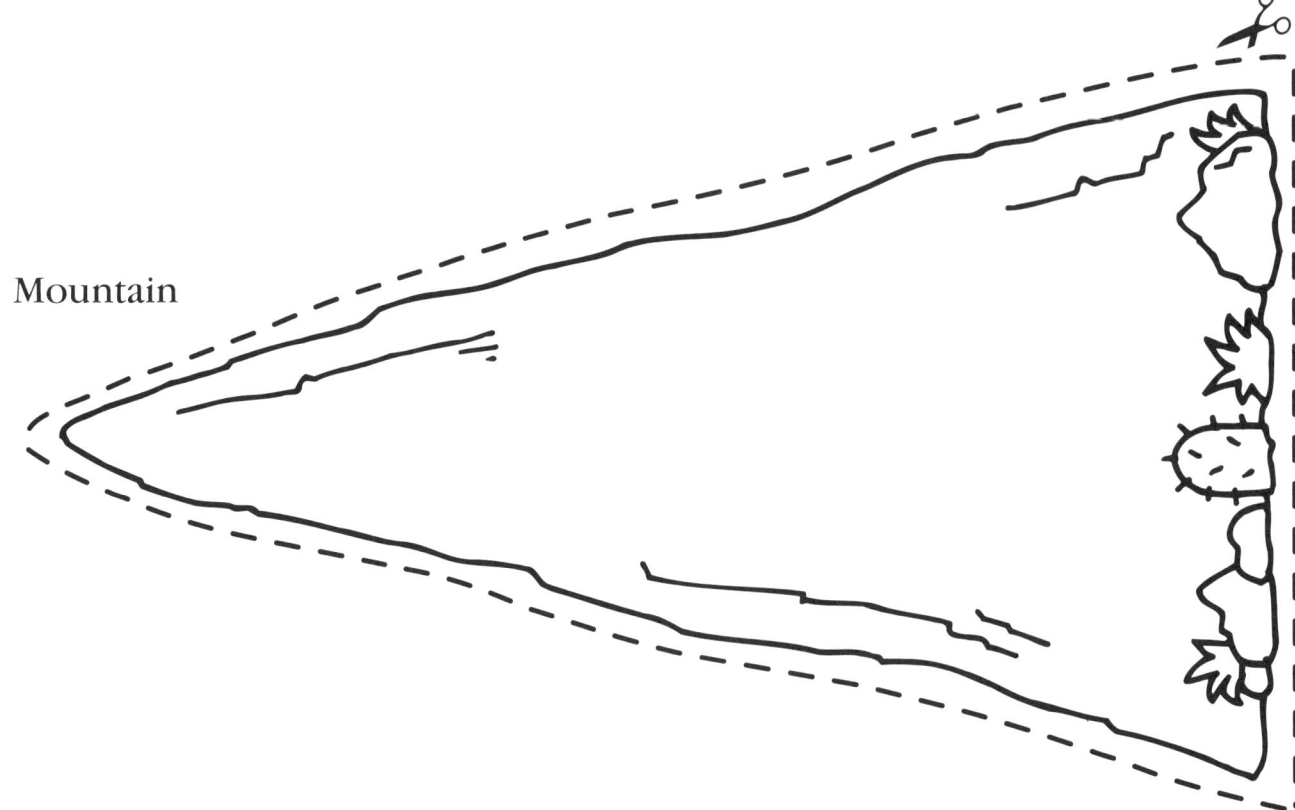

— Year A —

First week of Lent

Angel

Jesus

Fix tab to back of all card items to make them stand

Year A

Second week of Lent

Jerusalem

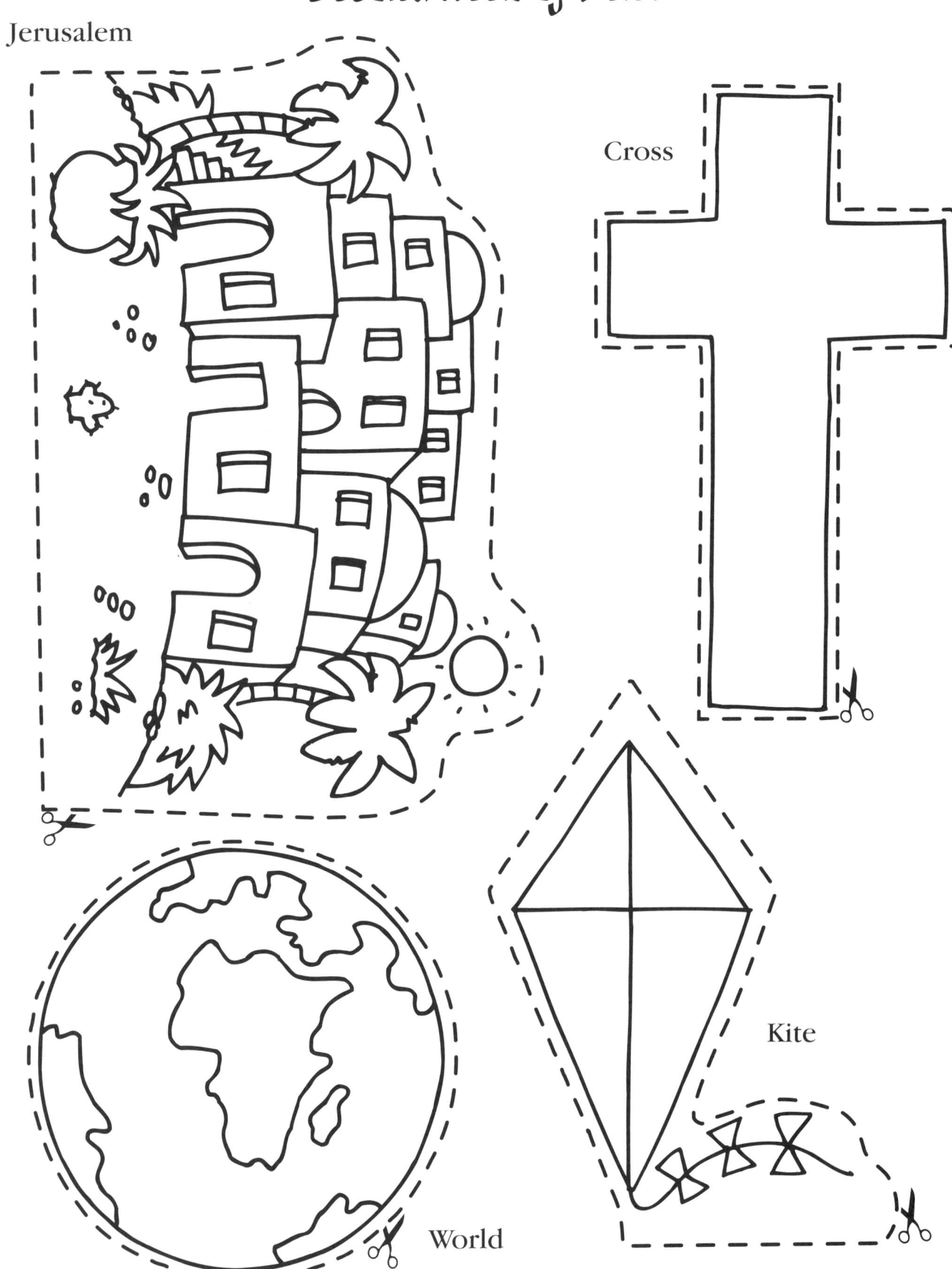

Cross

World

Kite

Year A

Third week of Lent

Samaritan woman

Crowd

Well

Waterfall

— Year A —

Fourth week of Lent

Blind man

Question mark

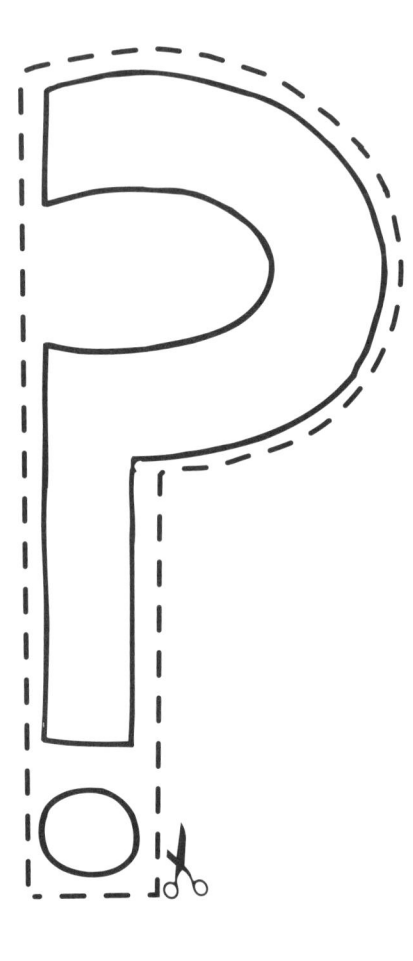

A pair of dark glasses

Year A

Fifth week of Lent

Mary and Martha

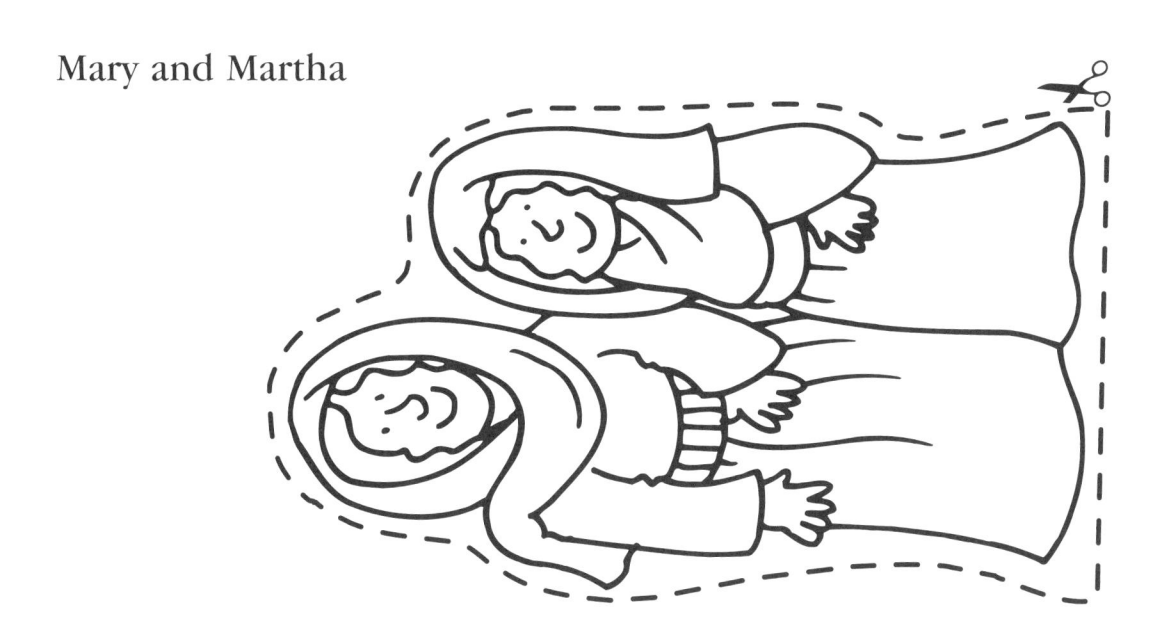

Crowd

Bethany signpost

Year A

Fifth week of Lent

Tomb

Stone

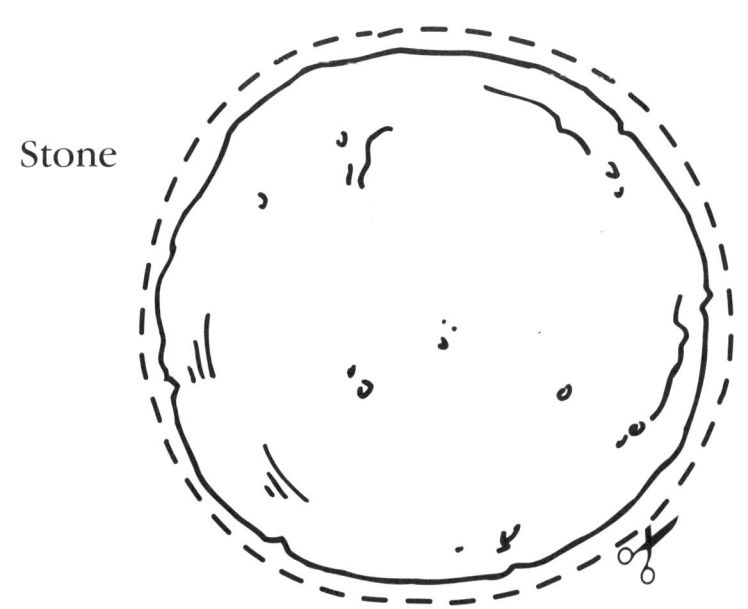

Year A

Fifth and Sixth week of Lent

Plate of Passover food

Judas

Disciples

Year A

Holy Week

Other Mary (and Salome)

Mary Magdalene

Galilee

Year B

First week of Lent

Dove

Wild animals

— Year B —

Third week of Lent

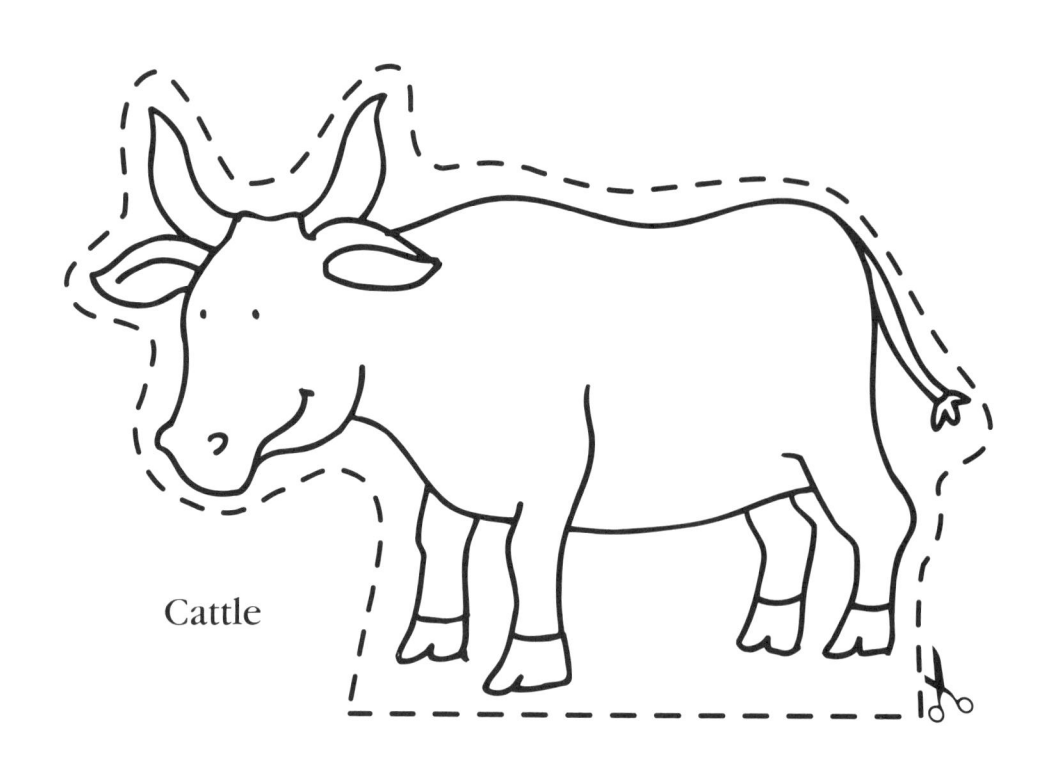

Sheep

Cattle

86 Reproduced with permission from *Play and Pray through Lent* published by BRF 2005 (1 84101 392 7)

Year B

Fourth week of Lent

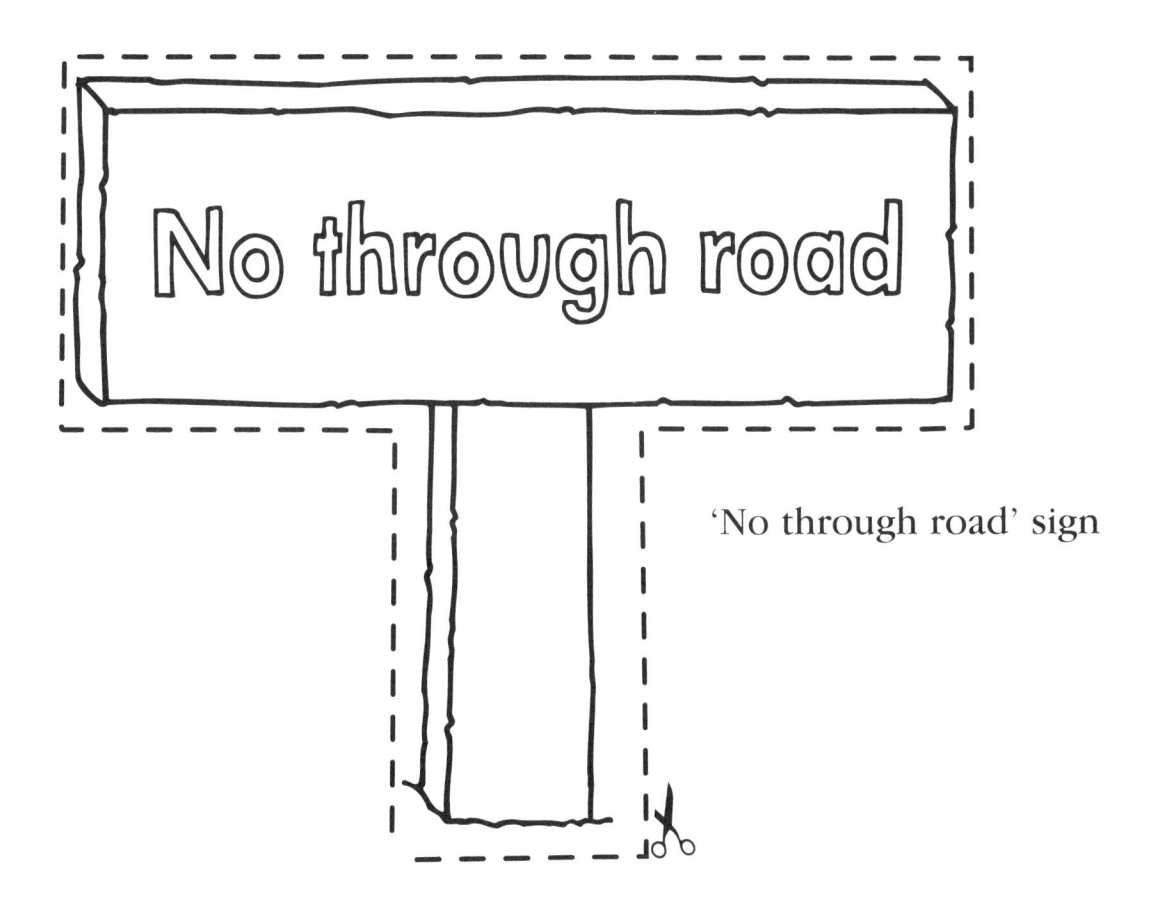

'No through road' sign

Year B

Sixth week of Lent

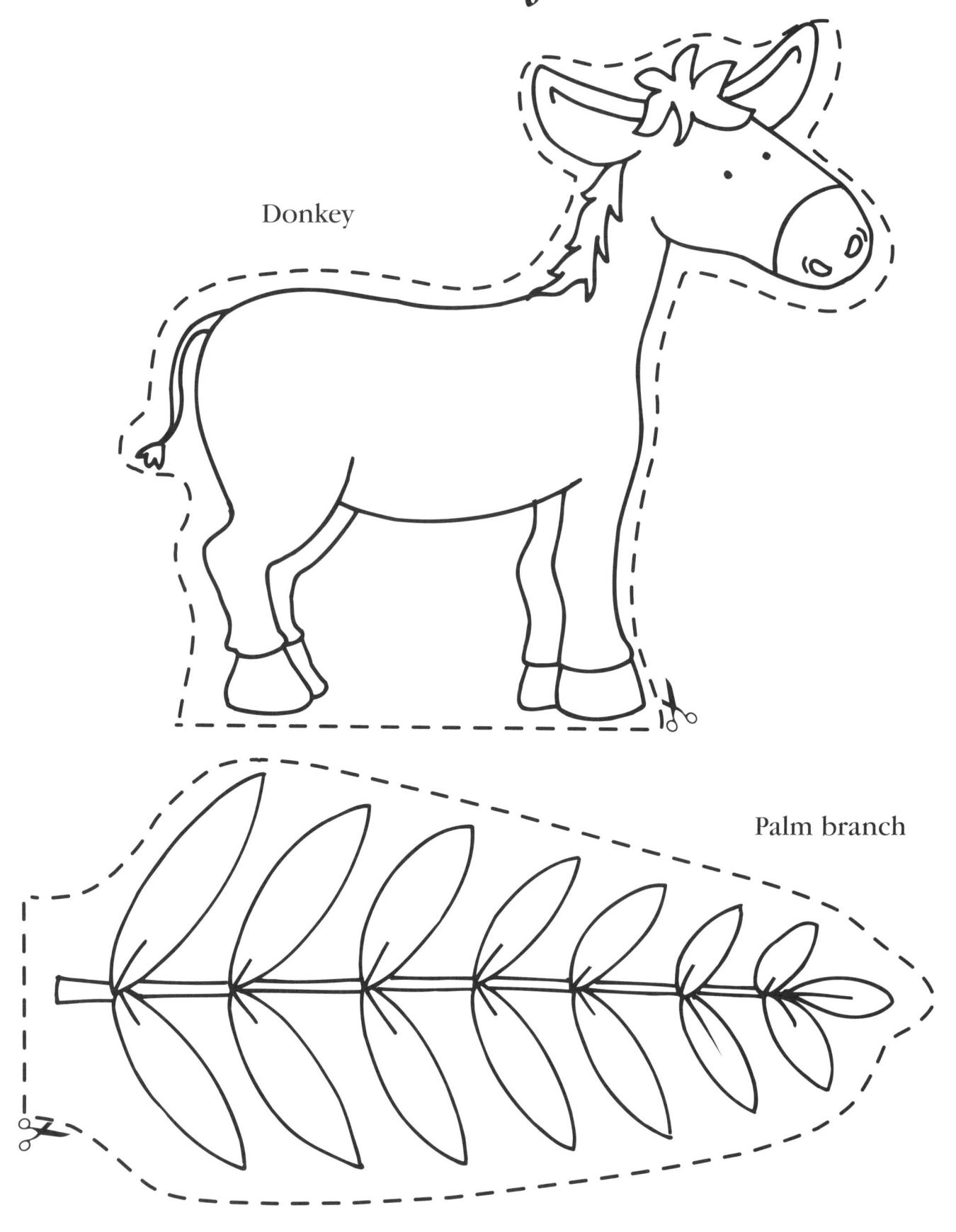

Donkey

Palm branch

88   Reproduced with permission from *Play and Pray through Lent* published by BRF 2005 (1 84101 392 7)

Year B

Holy Week

White-robed figure

Flowers

Year C

First week of Lent

Bible

―― Year C ――

Second week of Lent

Sword

Scroll

Chicks

Year C

Third week of Lent

'To God via Jesus' signpost

Empty basket

Fig tree

92 Reproduced with permission from *Play and Pray through Lent* published by BRF 2005 (1 84101 392 7)

Year C

Third week of Lent

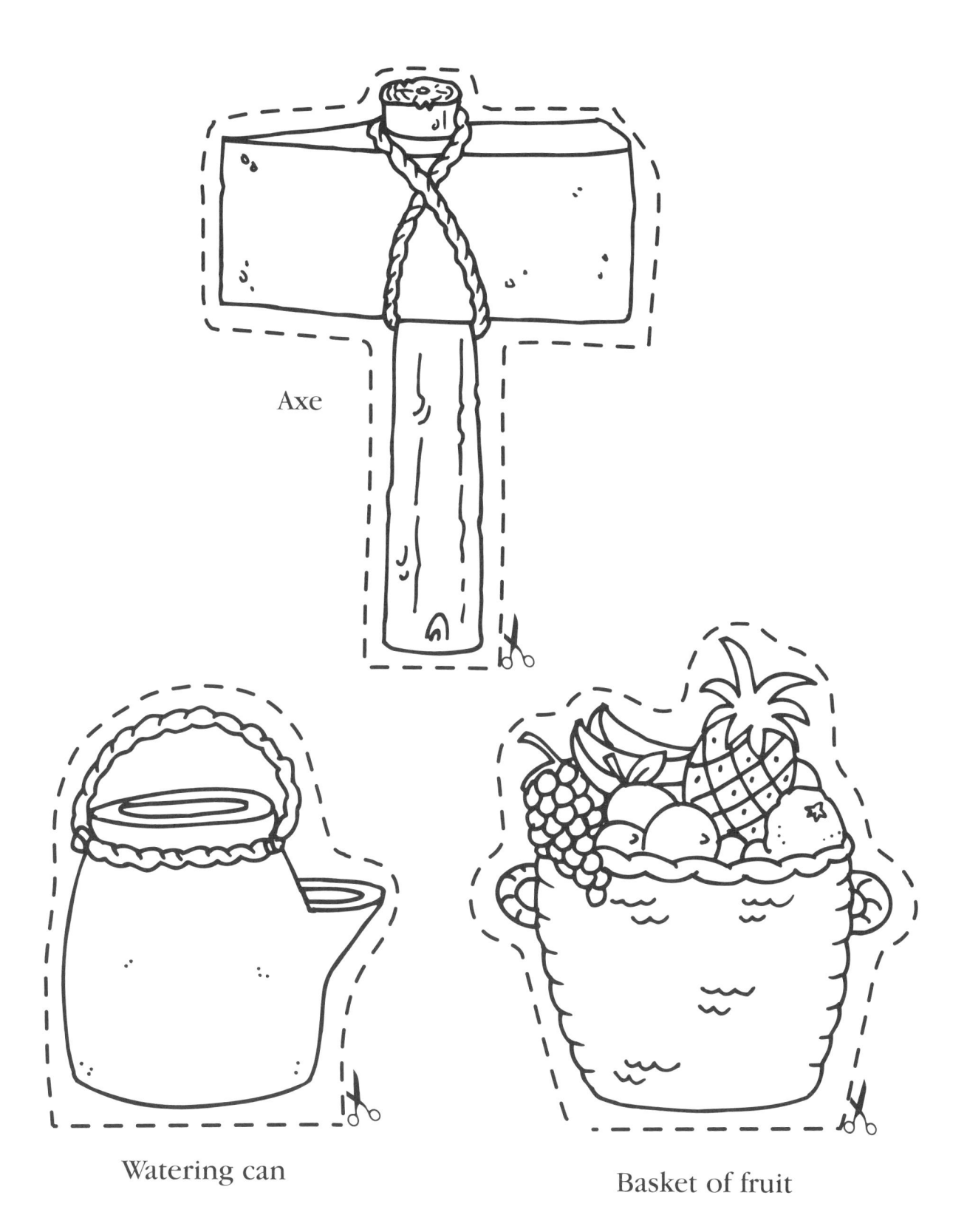

Axe

Watering can

Basket of fruit

Year C

Fourth week of Lent

Pig

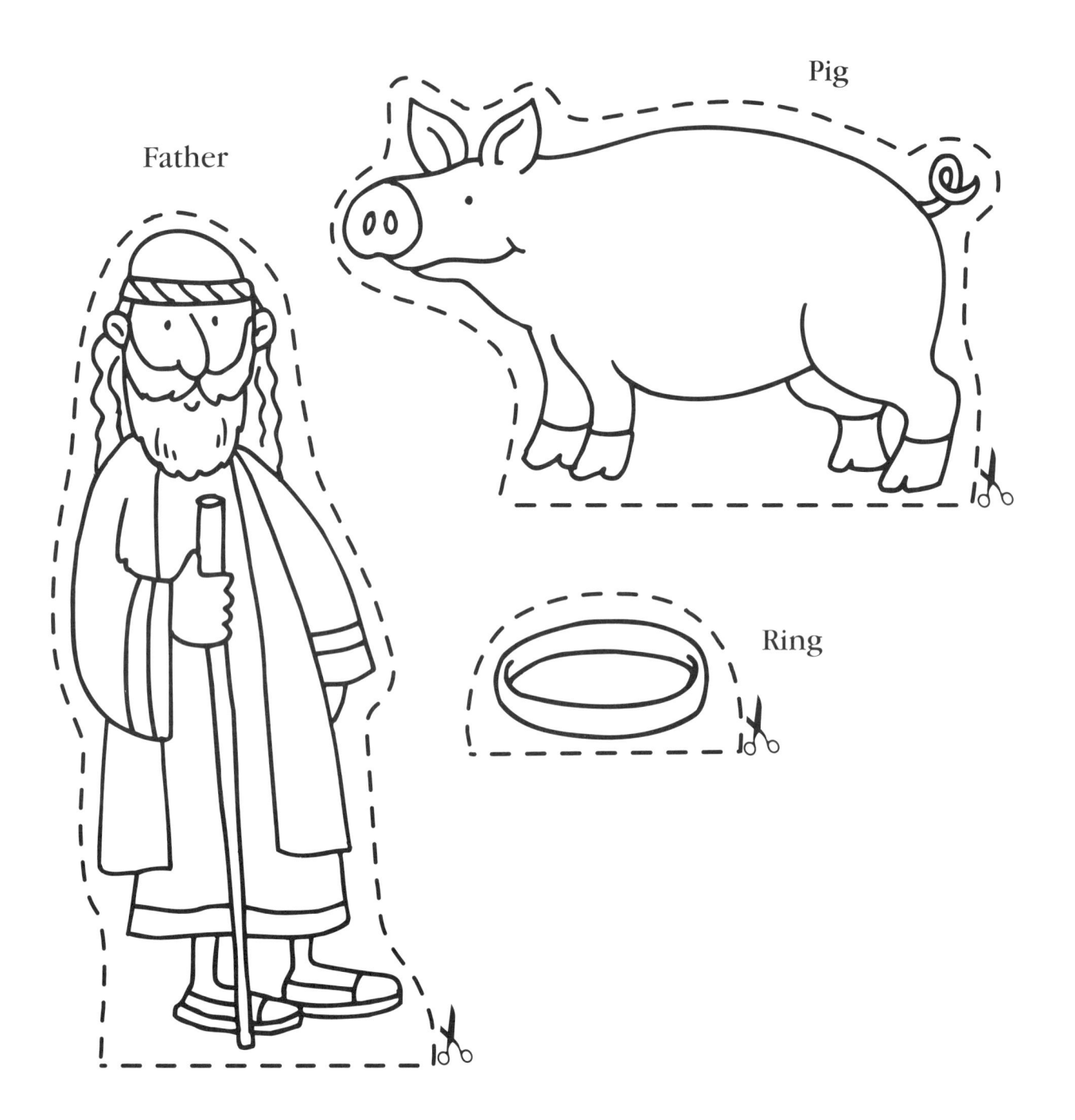

Father

Ring

Year C

Fifth week of Lent

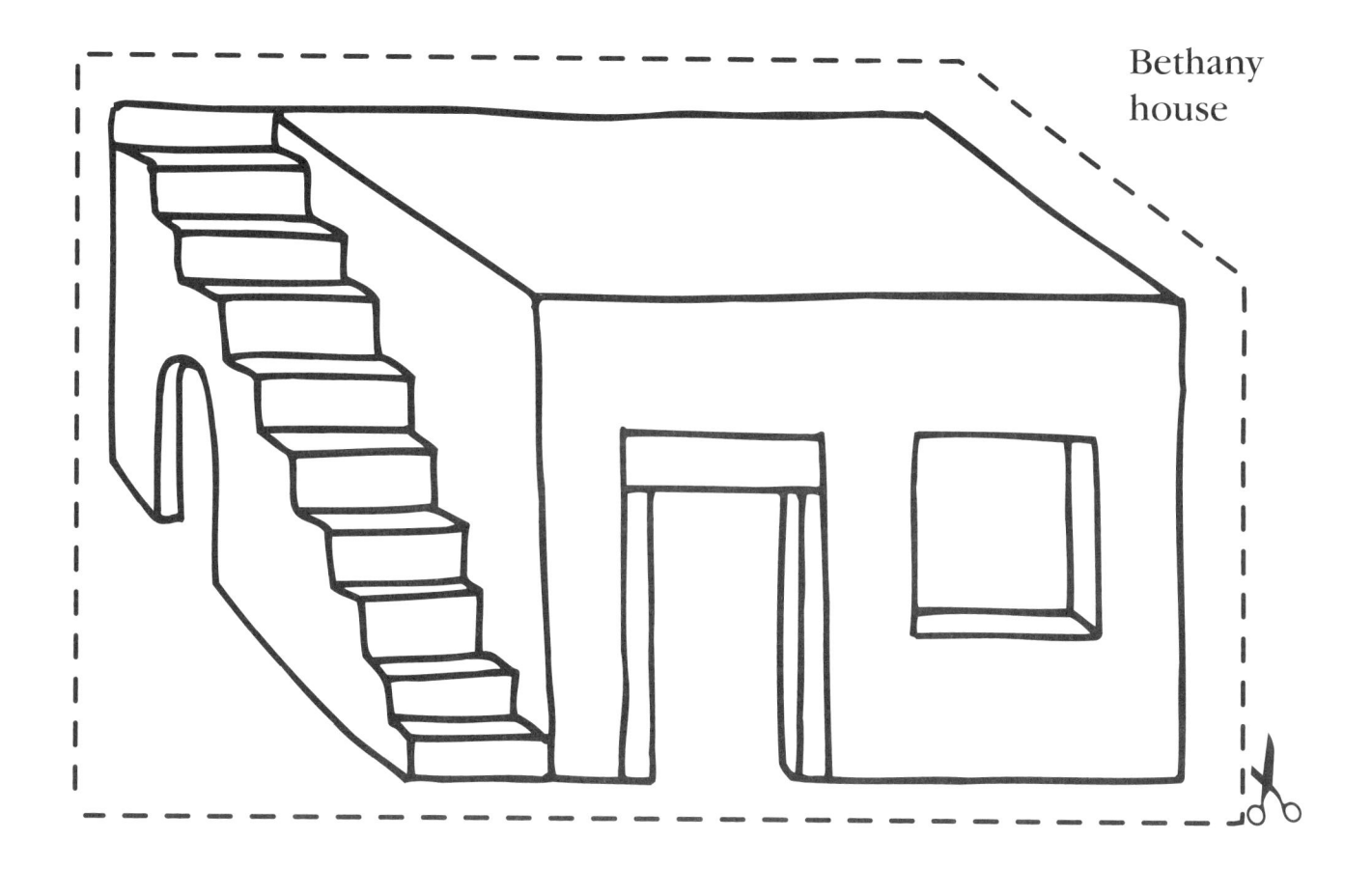

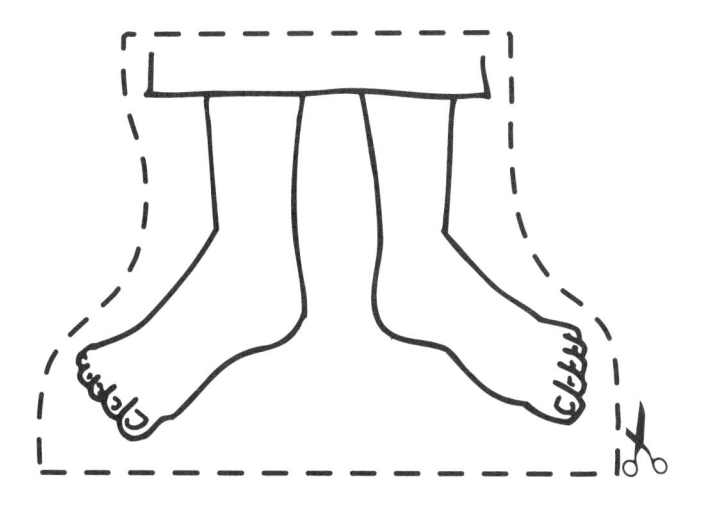

Bethany house

Feet

Denarius coin

— Year C —

Holy Week

Mary Magdalene

Peter

John

96